GENEALOGY IN THE COMPUTER AGE:
Understanding FamilySearch®

(Ancestral File, International Genealogical Index, and
U. S. Social Security Death Index)

Revised Edition

by Elizabeth L. Nichols, A. G.

Introduction

FamilySearch is a set of genealogical programs and data files on compact disc that can be used on a personal computer with a compact disc drive, or on a computer network. It is published by The Church of Jesus Christ of Latter-day Saints (LDS, Mormons, Genealogical Society of Utah) and is available at the Family History Library in Salt Lake City, Utah, and at most of its over 2,000 family history centers worldwide, and at many other libraries. (It is not generally available for personal purchase at this time.) Watch for updates to any or all of the following main files:

Ancestral File™

A pedigree-linked file sharing genealogies, focusing on people who are now deceased. Names are linked to parents, spouses, children, siblings (brothers and sisters), and other ancestors and descendants. Everyone is invited to contribute information to it. It allows for corrections and additions to be made and submitted on diskette, so that it can continually be improved. The current edition, released in 1993, contains 15 million names submitted through August 1992.

International Genealogical Index™ (IGI)

A file of over 200 million names from over 90 countries--many extracted directly from vital records; others submitted by relatives over a period of more than 150 years. Quality of the information varies, according to the source of input, which is identified in each entry. No links exist between one record and another, though names of parents or spouses are often included in an entry. The 1993 edition includes information through August 1993.

U. S. Social Security Death Index

A brief index of names of those whose deaths were reported to the Social Security Administration from 1962-1988. U.S. Government began to use computers in record keeping of these records in 1962. The file is made available through the Freedom of Information Act, and has been formatted to search as a part of FamilySearch. Only brief information is provided.

This book gives details and illustrations that lead you in a simple, organized way into finding, copying, and understanding the information in these files. It gives you the personal help of an expert who understands your needs and the strengths and limitations of the files.

CONTENTS

```
     FAMILYSEARCH MAIN MENU
Use ↓ ↑ keys to highlight options.
     Press Enter to select.

Getting Started
 A. Using the Computer

Finding Information
 B. Ancestral File
 C. International Genealogical Index
 D. U.S. Social Security Death Index
 E. Military Index
 F. Family History Library Catalog

Preparing Information
 G. TempleReady
 H. Personal Ancestral File
```

Firgure 1 Main Menu (FamilySearch)

The Library Catalog and Personal Ancestral File, which are also part of these computerized programs and files, will not be discussed in this publication. Only downloading records from Personal Ancestral File for submitting to Ancestral File, and uploading records into

Personal Ancestral File which were downloaded from FamilySearch will be discussed in this Part 1.

The genealogical resource files share many characteristics, and are therefore discussed in this single pamphlet.

How to Use this Pamphlet

This instruction is written to help beginners as well as intermediate and advanced users of FamilySearch.

The ideal way to use it is to already have seen FamilySearch and how it works, making the instruction easier to understand. If this is not feasible, the many illustrations included here will make it easy to understand. And understanding the concepts and principles as explained here will make it easier to follow the instructions given as part of FamilySearch.

First, read the glossary of terms (page 48), so you are familiar with the meaning of the words as they are used here. Next, look at the illustrations, so you can begin to have a mental image of what is meant. Then, read through the entire pamphlet, even though all of it does not yet make sense. This will help you acquire the background to understand the details.

Now you are ready to enjoy the instruction offered here, which will provide a foundation for a successful experience with FamilySearch, and the use of the wonderful technology available as it applies to the field of family history and genealogy. Use this pamphlet as a reference as you sit at the terminal using FamilySearch, or to assist you in teaching others.

GENERAL INFORMATION

An Overview

FamilySearch™ is a collection of computer programs and files which The Church of Jesus Christ of Latter-day Saints (LDS Church) is distributing to its family history centers throughout the United States and Canada. These materials eventually will be distributed to other countries as well. FamilySearch operates on a personal computer with a CD ROM drive or player for compact discs. FamilySearch makes a large part of the Family History Department's files available to people without their having to travel to Salt Lake City, Utah. (No access by modem is possible, nor is any presently planned.)

The following files are presently available at Salt Lake City and/or at family history centers:

1. Ancestral File™, 1992 edition, released 1993; containing 15 million names, pedigree-linked.

2. International Genealogical Index™ (IGI), 1993 edition; containing over 200 million names of individuals and couples.

3. Family History Library Catalog™;

4. Social Security Death Index, containing 39 million names (for persons whose deaths were reported 1962-1988, with a few earlier and later).

5. Military Index (listing U. S. citizens who died in Viet Nam and Korea).

A genealogy program for home computers, Personal Ancestral File®, is also part of the computer programs available.

For LDS Church members, the name clearance system (for submitting names for proxy LDS temple ordinances) is known as TempleReady™.

For those who are new at using a computer, there is also a short tutorial, along with further explanation of the copyright.

What to Expect

Computers at family history centers are used for a number of tasks and needs. Helping visitors use the data is a service offered as a courtesy. Policies and time frames on computer use are determined by the local Church leaders who administer the centers.

Wise use of the limited time available on the computer using FamilySearch is a must. The following descriptions and explanation of the files will enable you to use your computer time wisely.

COMMON CHARACTERISTICS

FamilySearch data files are on compact discs. Compact discs are like small records, similar to those used on a compact disc (CD) player to play music recordings. They are also used to store large amounts of information. A CD ROM drive is required to use compact discs, and special software is required to use the FamilySearch discs. The computer will tell you which disc to insert, based on the particular file you are using and the name you type into the blank space provided. The information will be displayed clearly on the screen (see Figure 2).

The International Genealogical Index has 33 discs in the 1993 edition; Ancestral File has four discs in the 1992 edition; and the Social Security Death Index, 1962-1988, has four discs. It is important that you have the correct compact disc for the correct file.

Finding the Information

All you need to do is type the name and sometimes the identifying date into the space provided, and press a function key (identified on the computer with an F in front of a number, such as F12). To have the request screen displayed, press the F4 key (see Figure 2). When you have typed in the information you want used in your search, press the F12 key to begin the search. You can begin a new search at any time by pressing the F4 key and typing in more or new information.

If you are not familiar with a computer keyboard and other aspects of using computers, see *The Genesis of Your Genealogy*, 3rd edition 1992. Pages 38-59 discuss computers and genealogy/family history from a beginners viewpoint.

```
                    Ancestral File B413                  07 MAR 1994
   Esc=Exit  F1=Help   F2=Print/copy   F3=Edit  F4=Search  F9=Sources  F10=Go-back


          SEARCH BY SURNAME AND GIVEN NAME
       Enter the information you want included in the search.

   Ancestor's name: James_____  HARVIE_____
                    Given Name(s)                  Surname (Last Name)

       Birth Year: 1746   (Optional)


                        INSERT COMPACT DISC

       Insert the following disc into drive G.

       Ancestral File                           WITHDRAWN
       Disc 4


    F12=
```

FIGURE 2 Request Screen (Ancestral File)

Names

1. *Surnames* (last names).

   • Surnames have a similar-name retrieval that allows for many spelling variations to be brought together. You can choose this option, or just have the exact spelling retrieved. Usually it is better to use the similar spelling option, because someone may have submitted the name spelled differently from what you expect.

   You may need to type in variations to have all similar names retrieved. Different formulas are used for different geographical areas and sometimes for different files (IGI, Ancestral File) for the same geographical area (United States, for example).

See also *Royalty* under Glossary to see how these names may be listed and retrieved.

A woman's record is generally found under her maiden surname in Ancestral File and International Genealogical Index (although she may be listed under any married surname). In the Social Security Death Index she is almost always listed under her married surname.

2. *Given names* (first and middle names) are also now retrieved on standard spellings. This is the first try and has some problems. For example, Bill and Billy are not retrieved with William. However, names such as Catherine and Katheryn; William, Wm, Wllm, Guillius; Thomas, Tho, Thos, are retrieved togther. This is a great advantage.

Middle given names are not used in the sort in the International Genealogical Index. This is new. They are arranged by surname, first given name, and year of event.

And sometimes all given names were not included.

If a person had three or more given names (John Albert Ernest, for example), often only the first two were typed into the computer. If the person was known by his third middle name (in this case, Ernest), it may be hard to recognize his entry, which could read John Albert). And a request for Albert Bolton will not retrieve an entry for John Albert Bolton.

In Ancestral File, names are more often written in full, including middle names. (So the problem here may be that a person was known by a middle name, which cannot retrieve the record.)

In the Social Security Death Index, almost always only the first given name is listed. If a person used a first initial and second given name, such as J. Milton Farwell, you may find it under J Farwell. If a person was known only by his middle name, you will not find him unless you know to look for him under his first given name or initial.

Given Name Arrangement for Some Areas. In the International Genealogical Index, there is a special given name arrangement for some countries, such as Denmark, Sweden, Finland, Norway, Iceland, and Wales, because of the patronymic naming customs, where surnames changed every generation. (See page 49.)

3. *Names of relatives* may be used to retrieve records.

You can usually retrieve a person's record by using the name of a relative. There are several ways to do this.

First, in the index listing for most of the files, the name of a relative is also included (see Figure 3).

Abbreviations are: Fa=father, Sp=spouse, Ch=child, Mo=mother.

In Ancestral File, if the name of the father is known, it will be listed in the index. The name of the spouse (if included in the file) can be seen by pressing the ENTER key. You will need to press the ENTER key a second time in order to view all of the information about that person, including additional marriages.

In the International Genealogical Index, for a marriage record, only the name of one spouse is given in a single record. There may be a separate record for any additional marriage, but there will be no link between the two marriage records. In a birth or christening record, the name of the father is visible in the index; the name of the mother, if given, can be viewed by pressing the ENTER key.

- In the International Genealogical Index, you can also bring together many of the records of the children, even when their given names are listed or spelled differently from what you may expect. This is done by using what is known as the Parent Index (see page 30).
The ways you can access one person's record through the record of a relative differ somewhat within the various files, but if the name of a relative is given in the file, you can use the relationship approach successfully. (The Social Security Death Index does not include the name of a relative.)

Example: My grandfather's name is John Albert Ernest Bolton, but he was known by Ernest or A. E. It is not possible to retrieve a name in any of the files by just typing in a middle given name (in this case, Ernest or Albert). If I limit myself to looking for Ernest Bolton or Albert Ernest Bolton, I will think the name is not there. But if I look for the name of his wife, Effie Mae Dewees or Deweese, in Ancestral File, her record will be linked to his record and I can retrieve his entire record. (I could also look for his father, mother, brother, sister, or child in Ancestral File, and probably retrieve his record through any of these relatives. Or I could begin with myself and move up the pedigree until I came to his record, since he is a direct ancestor, and then go to the family group record to find any brother or sister, or child.)

In the International Genealogical Index, I could look for the marriage record under his wife's name or the birth or christening record of one of his children and see how the husband or father's name is listed in that record. This same identification is then used to try to find an individual record for him, though a person listed as a parent in the International Genealogical Index does not always have an individual record listed there. (In the International Genealogical Index, the record of a spouse or child would not be linked to his record; I could only use the same spelling and listing of names to try to locate his individual record.)

4. *When the name is too long*. If a name is too long to be displayed on the screen, an asterisk (*) will appear. You can see the full name by pressing ENTER. If necessary, you can use the side-arrow key to scroll the screen to the right to see the name.

Occasionally you may find names of persons or places different from what you expect, because the Personal Ancestral File name fields are limited to 16 characters (letters). Most of the time this is enough,

but sometimes it is not and the person submitting the record must determine how to shorten or abbreviate the name. Although Ancestral File has the capacity to have more letters, the record will remain as it came into the system until someone changes it. This especially affects some Italian and German names.

5. *Retrieval by record number*. You can also retrieve a record in Ancestral File if you know the Ancestral File record identification number (AFN) assigned to that person. This option is listed as item C on the search menu.

When merges in records change an AFN, the old number is cross-referenced to the new number. (See Figure 20.)

Displaying the Information

An alphabetical list of names with brief details, arranged alphabetically by surname, will be displayed on the computer screen.

```
                        Ancestral File B413              31 MAR 1994
         Esc=Exit  F1=Help  F2=Print/copy  F3=Edit  F4=Search  F9=Sources  F1O=Go-back
        ┌─────────────┐  ┌──────────────┐  ┌──────────────┐  ┌─────────────────┐
        │  F5=Index   │  │  F6=Family   │  │  F7=Pedigree │  │  F8=Descendancy │
     ┌──┴─────────────┴──┴──────────────┴──┴──────────────┴──┴─────────────────┴──┐
     │                                                        ┌─────────────────┐ │
     │  Use ↓ ↑ PgDn and PgUp keys and press Enter for details.│  Enter=Details  │ │
     │                                                        └─────────────────┘ │
     │ ┌─Name (-Name Group-)──────────────────Born─Place────────Relative────────  │
     │↑│ -HARVEY-                                                                  │
     │ │    James HARVEY ...............    1743  ENGLAND      Fa:Charles HARVEY   │
     │ │    James HARVIE ..............     1746  SCOTLAND     Fa:James HARVIE     │
     │ │    James HARVEY ..............     1751               Fa:Thomas HARVEY    │
     │ │    James HARVEY ..............     1753  CONNECTICU   Fa:Joel HARVEY      │
     │ │    James HERVEY(HARVEY) .......    1753  ENGLAND      Fa:John HERVEY      │
     │ │    James HARVEY ..............     1754  CONNECTICU   Fa:Joseph HARVEY    │
     │ │    James HERVEY ..............    [1763]              Sp: MARSHALL        │
     │ │    James HARVEY ..............     1764  CONNECTICU   Fa:Joseph HARVEY    │
     │ │    James HARVIE (HARVEY) ......    1765  NOVA SCOTI   Fa:John HARVIE      │
     │ │    James HARVIE ..............     1765  SCOTLAND     Fa:Archibald HARVIE │
     │ │    James HARVEY ..............     1768  ENGLAND      Fa:John HARVEY      │
     │ │    James HARVIE ..............     1773  NOVA SCOTI   Fa:James HARVIE     │
     │ │    James HARVEY ..............     1777  ENGLAND      Sp:Diana BENNETT    │
     │↓│    James ARVIE  ..............ABT  1778               Sp:Susannah (Harvey) U│
     └─┴───────────────────────────────────────────────────────────────────────── │
     └───────────────────────────────────────────────────────────────────────────┘
```

FIGURE 3 Index Entries (Ancestral File)

You can select the name you want to know more about by using the down-arrow or up-arrow (keys with the tiny arrows on) to move the cursor to highlight the name you want. By pressing the ENTER key, more detail will be displayed, and you can decide if that is the name you are interested in. If you press ENTER a second time, more information may be displayed. Then, depending on the file you are using, other options are available (such as a pedigree chart in Ancestral File, or a Parent Index listing in the International Genealogical Index). See the descriptions of the individual files for more details.

Dates: Ancestral File and the International Genealogical Index (1992 and later editions) may contain exact or estimated dates. The Social Security Death Index contains only exact dates.

Estimated dates may appear with the term "Abt" (for about), or in brackets. The dates in brackets (see figure 3) have been estimated by the FamilySearch system, because the submitter gave no date. However, those with the term "abt" may have been provided by the submitter, or by a system. (See page 14 for more details.)

Making Copies

You may make paper copies, or download information for use on either a word processor or a personal computer software program that uses GEDCOM (such as the Personal Ancestral File) for all genealogical resource files. The process of taking the automated records from FamilySearch (or any computerized records) and placing them on a diskette to use in another computer program, without rekeying the information, is called downloading. Simple-to-follow instructions are displayed for each step.

For the International Genealogical Index and the Social Security Death Index, you prepare for downloading records by first placing them in a holding file. The holding file is accessed by pressing the F2 key (labeled print), and pressing the letter E (create or add to the holding file), and then with the highlight bar on the name you want to print or download, pressing ENTER).

When you are ready to print or download, return to the print menu (escape if you have been using the holding file, then press F2). Determine the type of copy you want to make. In the International Genealogical Index, select H to make a paper print or press the letter I to download to a diskette. Answer the questions as they

appear on the screen. You can choose whether to include LDS ordinance information in your download or paper printout by placing an X beside this option. (See page 34 for more information.)

For Ancestral File, you can download a single family group from a family group record screen; from a pedigree chart, you can choose to download information on all family members with the pedigree chart, or limit it to just the pedigree information (direct ancestors' records). You may also choose whether to include LDS ordinance dates.

In Ancestral File, you can print names and addresses of submitters on paper, but you cannot download this information onto a diskette at the present time. You must have the names of submitters on the screen to begin this process.

See pages 24, 42 for more information on downloading and uploading records from Ancestral File.

In the International Genealogical Index, no names of submitters are in the file, but the description and film number of the source used is given, and can be included in your printouts and downloads if you choose.

Paper printouts in draft form are on 8 1/2 x 11 inch paper that fits standard binders. Family Group records and pedigree charts, available from Ancestral File, are in a standard format for this size form, and can be printed with or without LDS temple ordinance dates. The same printouts from the Personal Ancestral File may be made in either 8 1/2 x 11 or 8 1/2 x 14 inch formats.

Obtaining Help

There are help messages for any screen or function that you are working with. Simply press the F1 key, and it will give you a choice of options. The help with the individual screen will be different for each screen, such as the pedigree chart in Ancestral File or the family group record, and even for a specific field on the screen, such as date, a place, or an LDS temple abbreviation. (See Figure 4.)

Personal Ancestral File also has help messages. To obtain help for specific fields on any screen, press the ALT and letter H keys at the same time.

Copyright

Most of the information in the FamilySearch files is copyrighted. This means that you can use it for your personal benefit, but no one can lawfully sell it. This is to protect all of us who have submitted information to the files. We give our information to Ancestral File; it would not be fair for someone to sell it. The copyright, then, is to prevent this from happening. Anyone who has submitted information can continue to use that information in any way desired.

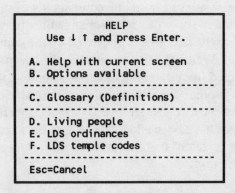

FIGURE 4 Help Menu (Ancestral File)

The one exception to the copyright is the Social Security Death Index. This information, which comes from the federal government, is made available through the Freedom of Information Act and cannot be copyrighted.

ANCESTRAL FILE

Ancestral File is the heart of FamilySearch. It is pedigree-linked—that is, it shows individual records linked to the records of parents, spouses, children, and siblings (brothers and sisters). The links may also extend to grandparents (for as many generations as have been submitted), granduncles, grandaunts, cousins, and in-laws.

Record Elements

The amount of information contained in an Ancestral File record depends on several factors. There are three types of records:

1. *Deceased persons.* Full genealogical and LDS ordinance detail (whatever has been submitted) is displayed.

   The amount of information depends on what has been submitted. Sometimes family groups where the person is listed as a parent and also as a child have been submitted, but sometimes only the family

group where he is listed as a parent or the one where he is listed as a child has been submitted, and sometimes only a pedigree entry has come in. The file reflects what has been submitted specifically for the Ancestral File, not what may be contained in other Family History Department files.

2. *Living persons.* These are separated into two types:

   • Living persons who are members of The Church of Jesus Christ of Latter-day Saints and whose baptism date was included in the record submitted for Ancestral File. These persons have a legal connection with the LDS Church. The NAME of the person will be displayed, showing links to his family members, but no genealogical or ordinance detail will be displayed.

   • Living persons who are NOT members of the LDS Church. The word LIVING will be displayed, showing the links of the records into pedigrees and family groups. No name will be listed.

   Thus, rights of privacy are preserved.

A living person is defined as one who was born within the past 95 years and for whom no death date has been submitted to Ancestral File.

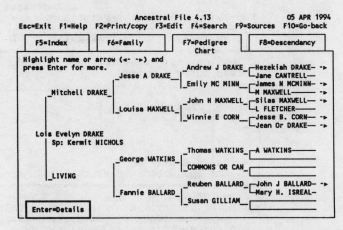

FIGURE 5 Records that display only the word LIVING link generations (Ancestral File)

Displays

1. *Arrangement.* The information can be displayed in
   • An alphabetical index, similar to a telephone directory, where names are arranged by surname (see Figure 3). You may choose to see them with only the exact spelling of the surname, or you can have similar surnames also retrieved and

displayed. Following the surname, names are sorted by

- Given name

- Year of birth or christening;

- Second given name or initial (Ancestral File only)

- Year of birth or christening.

  Example, Ancestral File

  John Smith . . . . b. 1790

  John Smith . . . . b. 1810

  John Smith . . . . b. 1880

  John A. Smith . . . . b. 1816

  John Andrew Smith . . . . b. 1795

The IGI ignores middle names and initials.

- One level of the place of birth will be listed. For example, in the United States, the state will be displayed (up to 10 letters); in most countries, only the name of the country is shown. Pressing the ENTER key will display more detail.

2. The top of the screen will tell you if there is a pedigree chart, and/or family group or descendancy chart in the file for that person.

If the word PEDIGREE shows next to the F7 at the top of the screen (see Figure 3), you can view the pedigree by pressing the key marked F7. It will be necessary to change compact discs after pressing the F7 key, and the screen will tell you which disc to insert. Sometimes an entire five-generation pedigree will be displayed from one compact disc, but sometimes you will need to change the disc several times as the pedigree is displayed on the computer screen. Watch the screen or when the compact disc is ejected from the drive to know when you need to insert another disc. It may almost immediately request the disc just removed. When corrections or lineages have been added, the computer sometimes needs to "fetch" that information from storage on another disc.

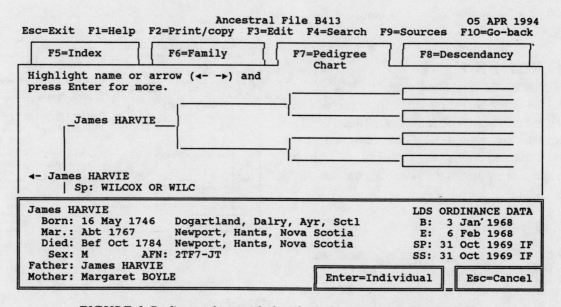

FIGURE 6 Pedigree chart with detail window open (Ancestral File)

After the pedigree chart is displayed, press ENTER to view more detail on any person. Pressing the ENTER key a second time may reveal additional detail, such as the names and marriage detail of additional spouses. Pressing the ESC key will remove the detail "window" from the screen. You can move from one ancestor to another by use of the arrow keys.

If a pedigree extends beyond one chart, arrows indicate this by pointing to the right. To view the extended pedigree, place the cursor on the arrow, and press ENTER. An arrow to the left of the name displayed as number 1 means that person has descendants listed in the file.

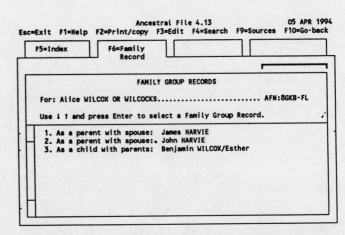

FIGURE 8 *Lists all family groups in which this person is included as a parent or as a child (Ancestral File).*

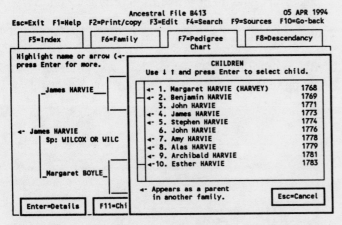

FIGURE 7 *Brief family group displayed by pressing F11 (Ancestral File)*

3. While viewing the pedigree chart, if the bottom of the screen shows an F11, there is a family group (more children) for this couple listed in the file. Press the F11 key and you can see a brief list of them with the year of birth for each child. If you want to see more detail press either the F6 key to take you to a family group record for this couple or an F7 key to go to a pedigree chart. You can then press ENTER and see all the details for each person. To move to another display for that person, you must place the highlight bar on the person's name before pressing F6 or F7.

When you press F6, you will first see a screen listing all family groups that include that person. The person may be listed as a child and as a parent. If he or she was married more than once, all spouses whose records have been submitted and linked to that person will be listed. If all marriages include the date of marriage, the marriages will be listed in chronological order. However, if one does not include a date of marriage, it is listed last. (In this case, Alice Wilcox was married first to James Harvie, and after his death married his cousin John Harvie who also had been widowed. Because there is no marriage date for her marriage to James Harvie, it is listed last even though it was her first marriage.) When printed copies of family groups are made, information on additional marriages print at the end of the family group record.

Sometimes a person may be listed in more than one family as a child (adopted or sealed into one family but a bloodline child to a different parent or set of parents). More often, however, at present the additional family as a child may be caused by a duplicate record that needs to be merged for one parent or set of parents.

You can choose to view the detail of any one of these families by moving the highlight bar to the name of the parent or spouse and pressing ENTER.

After the family group is displayed, and you have pressed ENTER once to see more detail for the husband (or any person listed on the screen), you can move the cursor down by using the arrow key, and it will show the detail for the next person in the family. You can do this with the window open, and it will display the detail for the next family member. You can also move to another display for that person by placing the highlight bar on that name and pressing another function key; for example, the F7 key will take you to a pedigree chart beginning with that person.

4. *Go Back.* To see a list of the displays you have already looked at, press the F10 key. To return to any one of these, place the highlight bar on that line and press ENTER. You will go immediately to that display, without having to wait. (The computer has retained that information in its buffer or memory.) This can be a real timesaver.

5. *Descendancy Chart.* Ancestral File will display or print a limited number of generations of descendants. The word DESCENDANCY appears at the top of the screen if there is a marriage listed for the person.

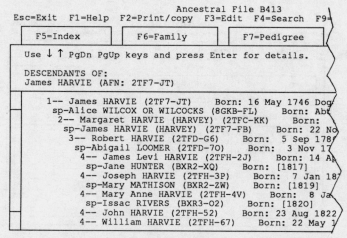

FIGURE 9 Descendancy Chart (Ancestral File)

The number to the left of the name on a descendancy chart is the generation number. The person whose descendants are listed is generation number 1, his or her children are all generation number 2, the grandchildren are all generation number 3, etc. The spouse of each person is listed, if their records are included in Ancestral File and linked to the person.

6. *Individual record.* There are four possible levels of individual detail:

- The index, where the names are listed (see Figure 3).

- By pressing ENTER while in the index, slightly more detail is displayed.

- After you have made a selection and left the index disc, more detail is displayed when you press the ENTER key.

- By pressing the ENTER key a second time, all detail for that person will be displayed (use the down arrow key and scroll down to view all of the detail).

Making Copies

You can select the copying option you want in the following ways:

1. To make a paper copy or download for use with a word processor, press A.

2. To make a paper printout of the names of your ancestors who do not have LDS ordinance dates included in their record, press B (for members of The Church of Jesus Christ of Latter-day Saints).

3. To copy for use with a genealogy computer program using GEDCOM (such as the Personal Ancestral File), press C.

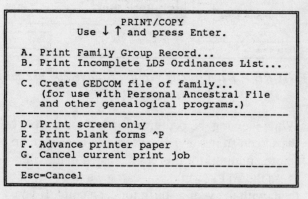

FIGURE 10 Print/Copy Menu (Ancestral File)

4. To make a copy of what you presently see on the screen, press D.

5. To print a blank pedigree chart or family group record, press E.

6. To advance the paper in the printer so you can tear off the copies you have made, press F.

7. To change your mind and cancel a request you have made, press G.

When you select option A, Print Pedigree Chart, you will see another menu which includes a number of choices.

The first block allows you these choices:

- How many generations you want on your pedigree chart (four generations lists only 15 names, but includes genealogical detail on all of them; five generations includes 31 names, but names only for numbers 16-31 and place names may need to be abbreviated for the other names on the chart; six generations will list 64 names, but information is abbreviated for all generations and names only are listed for numbers 32-64.)

```
                         Ancestral File B413                 07 MAR 1994
Esc=Exit  F1=Help  F2=Print/copy  F3=Edit  F4=Search  F9=Sources  F10=Go-back

                         PRINT PEDIGREE CHART
   Use ↓ ↑ and press Enter to change selections.  Press F12 to finalize.

  CHART TYPE                              Pedigree of                  AFN
     4 Generations per page               Margaret HARVIE (HARVEY)     2TFC-KK
     5 Generations per page
     6 Generations per page
                                          OUTPUT DEVICE
  OPTIONS                                    Send to printer
  [X] Ancestral File Numbers (AFN)           Print to diskette
  [ ] Related Family Group Records           (Printing to diskette creates
      Warning: This option may                an ASCII text file that can
      produce more than 20 printed            be used with most word
      pages.                                  processing programs.)
  [ ] Ped. Chart Reference Numbers

  An X indicates item is selected.        F12=Okay              Esc=Cancel
```

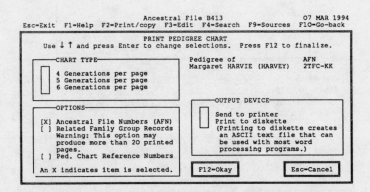

FIGURE 11 Additional choices for printing, or for downloading in ASCII; use the output device option on this menu to download onto diskette for use in a word processor (Ancestral File)

- Whether to list the AFN (Ancestral File Number) on the chart.
- To download records for use in a word processor (ASCII). Place an X in front of this option to select it.
- To have records prepared for a laser printer (if the center has such a possibility, or if you want to take it elsewhere and have it printed). The prints you make at the computer workstation will be draft quality only.

The second block allows you to choose whether you want your paper printouts to include the Ancestral File record number (AFN). If you do, leave the X; if you do not, press ENTER and the X will disappear.

The third block allows you to choose to make a copy of the data on the diskette for use on a word processor.

When you have indicated your choices for each item (whether it is a paper print or a download to diskette), press the F12 key. (Pressing the ESC key will take you back to a previous screen, and allow you to make another choice.)

If you press F12 from the above screen (Figure 11), the following menu will appear:

```
             RELATED FAMILY GROUP RECORDS

  Warning: This option will print Family
  Group Records for ALL of the couples on
  the Pedigree Chart and can produce more
  than 20 printed pages.  (You may print
  Family Group Records from the Family
  Record screen under the F6 option.)

       Use ↓ ↑ and press Enter to select.

  A. Print family groups with LDS dates
  B. Print family groups without LDS dates

 ------------------------------------------
 Esc=Cancel                    F12=Continue
```

FIGURE 12 Choose whether to include complete family groups and/or LDS ordinance detail in printing and word processor downloads (Ancestral File)

- Press A if you only want the pedigree printed.
- Press B to include family groups with LDS ordinance dates
- Press C to include family groups but omit LDS ordinance dates.
- Press the F12 key when you have indicated your selections.

For downloading in GEDCOM format, press C option, and follow the instructions.

```
     Include all family members
     Pedigree only

  OPTIONS
  [X] LDS Ordinance Dates
  [ ] Instructions (README.GIS)

  An X indicates item is selected.

  F12=Okay                 Esc=Cancel
```

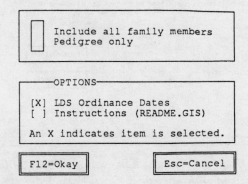

FIGURE 13 Choose whether to include all family members, LDS ordinance detail, and the README instructions in downloading records in the GEDCOM format (Ancestral File)

You can choose whether to include only the pedigree, or to also include records for all family members, and whether to include LDS ordinance dates.

There is also a README file that you can download and take home and read, which includes instructions for using the GEDCOM file.

Place an X in front of the options you want, then make sure it is displayed before you press the F12 key to finalize your request.

The system will prompt you when to insert a diskette. (You may be able to purchase these from the family history center, or it may be necessary for you to bring your own.) Labels are available from your family history center, preprinted to remind you of the copyright on the material you download.

You will then be asked to name your GEDCOM file (see Figure 14). This can be any word or combination of words and numbers up to 8 characters. In this case, we will call the first GEDCOM file HARVIE. (The second file, which can be on the same diskette can be called HARVIE1, HARVIE2, WILCOX, or whatever name we may choose.) If you choose a name that you have already used, the computer will tell you this, and ask if you want to add records to the existing GEDCOM file, or begin a new file. If you want to begin a new file, you must change the name in some way.

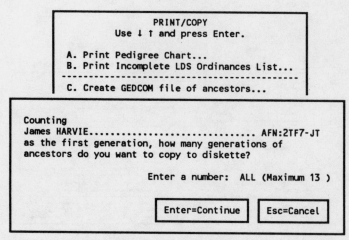

FIGURE 15 Selecting the number of generations to download (Ancestral File)

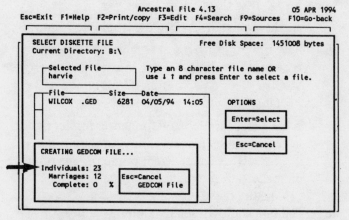

FIGURE 16 Creating the GEDCOM file (Ancestral File)

The screen will next tell you that the file is being checked. This makes sure the links for additional marriages are preserved.

When the screen returns to the print menu (Figure 10), the downloading process is complete. You can either remove your diskette or download another group of records to the same diskette.

(See page 42 for uploading GEDCOM records.)

Content

1. The Ancestral File has been created from:

   - The four-generation submissions requested from families of The Church of Jesus Christ of Latter-day Saints beginning in 1978.

   - Many extended lineages from family organizations and individuals.

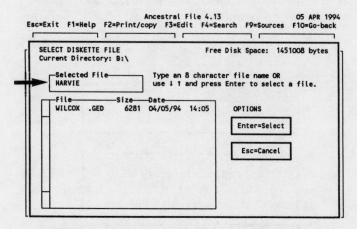

FIGURE 14 You must name your GEDCOM file (diskette used with Ancestral File GEDCOM download)

Press the ENTER key when you have typed in a name for your file.

The next screen will allow you to tell the computer how many generations to include. The maximum is usually thirteen generations at one time. Press the ENTER key to continue. The computer will now retrieve these records, organize them, and download them onto the diskette (see Figure 15).

- The Royalty and Medieval Identification Unit of the Family History Department.
- Records from families and individuals who are not members of the LDS Church, received since 1978.

In 1978 families of the LDS Church were asked to work together and verify and document their first four generations, beginning with the oldest living family members as names number 1 on the pedigree chart. They were asked to submit one pedigree chart and its associated seven family group records. Many responded, and many submitted additional generations at that time, and others have done so since then.

2. *Limitations*. Four-generation submissions made earlier than 1978 are NOT included in Ancestral File. Other collections of family group records and/or pedigree charts within the files of the Family History Department are NOT presently included. (This means that people can submit the most correct and current information to form the base of Ancestral File. Although corrections can be made to the data, it is far better to begin with correct information. Many families have discovered errors in the information that had been previously submitted to some files.)

3. *Duplication*. In theory, all records for a particular person have been brought together into a single record. In reality, this has not yet happened in all cases. The formula for matching and merging entries tries to be conservative and to avoid mis-merges (though, regrettably, some of these are found in the file, and your help is needed to identify and request correction on them). You will find cases where two or more records for the same person exist and need to be merged. Your help is needed to help perfect and complete the information in the file. **The correction feature allows this to be done more easily (see below).**

Even with its imperfections, consider the marvel of what the computer has been made to do. Many records have been submitted by 75 (and more) different submitters. The system has brought these together into one record (sometimes with manual help from correction staff members). Sometimes 69 of 70 have merged, but one did not. To understand merging, realize that to the computer, one letter different makes it a different name. To have 69 of the 70 records merged into one is a great advantage to the file users.

Understanding the Data

1. *Accuracy*. Accuracy of information is the responsibility of the various submitters. The Family History Department is NOT responsible for correctness of the data submitted. Regrettably, the merging process sometimes takes less correct information because it was submitted first, and keeps it until a special request is made for a correction. If another submission comes in with the incorrect information repeated, it can create additional duplicate records or other data problems.

2. *Building the File*. Care was used to avoid problems in the early stages of building the file. When the first entries were brought together, the formula used by the computer was based on these guidelines:

- Information submitted on a family group record where a person was listed as parent was given highest priority. (The assumption was that a parent on a family group record was a direct ancestor of the submitter, and in most cases research would be more carefully done on direct ancestors.)

- If no record for a person as a parent (parent entry) was submitted, an entry listing him as a child was given priority.

- If no parent or child entry was submitted, then a pedigree entry (which contains less information) was used as priority information. When two or more parent entries (or child entries with no parent entry) were received, the number of sources listed on the family group record were counted and the one listing the most sources was given priority.

This formula was not perfect. Sometimes the submitter listed only "family records" as a source, when in reality he had carefully documented every item in his own records. But as a rule of thumb for the base file, this procedure did allow some reason for what information was chosen to be listed. (These guidelines are no longer followed.)

For each individual submission, the three (or more) entries for a person (where the same person was listed as a parent on one or more family group records, as a child on another, and on the pedigree chart), were coded (by volunteers) to indicate they were the same person, typed into the computer (by other volunteers), and merged by the computer based on these codes. This worked in most cases. However, occasionally a mistake was made in the coding or typing, resulting in errors in the data. And since it was not done by family members, the errors could not be identified.

If a submitter sent in more than one pedigree chart, even in the same submission, each chart was considered separately. For example, if Andrew Harvie is listed as name 26 on my first five-generation pedigree chart, with no details, only his name, he may also be listed as name 1 on an additional chart. The second pedigree chart would list his genealogical details, along with his ancestors. Thus, Andrew Harvie would be listed in two different submissions from me. If I had submitted only one family group record for him, a decision had to be made as to which submission would include it.

Let's say that the family group record was included with the submission where his name appeared as 1 (the second pedigree chart). This means that only his name was listed on the first pedigree chart, along with the name of his spouse, and the name and genealogical detail of a child. His name could become a name-only from that first pedigree chart, and the linkage of his ancestors to his descendants was lost. When the name-only records were converted to full records, with estimated dates and places, the data could be so different that it would not merge. Until someone manually made a correction to the file, the duplication would remain, with the generations not linked. When they are linked, it appears as if the same person had submitted the information twice, when in fact only one submission may have been made containing more than one pedigree chart.

"Name-only" records were created when no family group record or continuation pedigree chart was submitted for those persons who were listed as:

- Names 16-31 on a five-generation pedigree chart (space for names only);

- Names of parents of the husband or wife on a family group record where no space was provided for dates or places;

- The spouse of a child on a family group record, these names originally became "name only" records.

The names were simply attached to their relative's record, but did not have any dates or places associated with them, and had no record identification number (AFN). In the first edition (October 1989) of Ancestral File, these names are listed with a PRE or ABT date. The file contained about two and a half million of these name-only entries.

These records may now appear with brackets to indicate that the system generated dates for them.

Ancestral File no longer carries name-only records. These records have been assigned estimated dates, and linked to the record of the spouse or child. This is important in understanding the data, because it does NOT mean the submitter did not have exact dates and places for the person, but only that the forms as submitted did not provide places for that information and it was therefore not submitted. Before conducting research or using the information in other ways, check with the submitters! They may already have done the research and have all the information verified and complete and LDS ordinances may already be done. One purpose of the file is to increase coordination and reduce duplication of effort, but communication is required to make it work most efficiently.

These estimated dates and places will often hinder the names from merging with the correct information when it is submitted. People can often see that the records pertain to the same individual, but the computer cannot. Therefore, you may need to help by identifying the duplicate records, and merging them using the edit key (F3).

3. *Guidelines Used for Estimating the Dates.* Any formula for estimating dates is imperfect and will result in many years difference from the actual dates for many of the records. One man said he had one son who married at the age of 30 and another who married at the age of 18; take the average of the two and you have the general guidelines, but you are far away from the birth years of both men.

For example, the 1989 edition of Ancestral File shows seven records for Prudence Marston, when they all refer to the same person. The birth years are: abt 1594, [1596], [1619], [1621], 1622, 1630, [1632], Pre-1681. She was married twice--years apart, plus having dates estimated from the birth records of her children (who were also born years apart). Only someone familiar with the family could recognize that these records all refer to the same person.

So be aware that the file may show dates and even places that do not match the facts, but the record may still refer to your ancestor. On the other hand, similar names and dates do not always mean it is the same person. Look at the names and dates for relatives and consider everything before deciding. If you have complete information, please help perfect the file. (It would be helpful if the family coordinated on who was going to correct which record. Then all the records could be evaluated and updated where needed, but only once.)

In Ancestral File different formulas have been used at different times and phases of the creation of the file, so there is not one standard for estimating dates. There are also different bases for estimated dates. For birth: those using a spouse's date of birth, those using the marriage date, those using a child's birth, and those using a sibling's (brother or sister) date of birth.

During the initial load, the husband was always estimated to be four years older than the wife (parents were assumed to be age 22 for the mother and age 26 for the father when the oldest child was born, or when any individual child was listed); children were assumed to be two years apart when a sibling's date was used; when the marriage date was used, husband was assumed to be 25 and the wife 21 years.

However, when the name-only entries were converted to records, if the spouse already had an Ancestral File record, the name-only was linked to the spouse's record and given as an estimated birth year the same year as the spouse was born.

Remember that an *estimated* (about, approximated) date is different from a calculated date (though the terms are sometimes mistakenly used interchangeably). A calculated date should come from a definite age at a certain time, that allows you to calculate the year of birth. This is true of census records (age 45 in 1850, allowing a *calculated* year of birth of 1805), or death records that give an age (age 78 in 1792, calculated year of birth as 1714). An estimated (about) date is simply guessed at, based on certain criteria. (For example, assuming that a person married at the "average" age, that it is the first marriage, that the child is the first child, etc.)

You may find the same person in Ancestral File and the International Genealogical Index with different estimated dates (even when the dates in both files are generated by the computer). And when the submitter estimated the dates before submitting the information, he or she may have used an even different basis for the estimation.

This means that you must be alert to recognize your relative's record even when the dates are not the same.

(Beginning in late 1990, the same formula for estimating dates is used for Ancestral File and the names clearance files that are indexed in the International Genealogical Index. Therefore, for records submitted after that date that are missing a birth year causing the computer to assign an estimated one, the same year is assigned in both files. Dates will be estimated to show four years difference in the birth years for the husband and the wife.)

4. *LDS Dates.* Remember too that when LDS families were asked to submit seven family group records, the old style family group form did not provide a space for the date the husband and wife on the form were each sealed to their parents, or for when a child listed on the form was sealed to a spouse. The absence of such a sealing date, therefore, does not mean that it has not been done. And since the pre-1970 temple sealing records are not yet in the International Genealogical Index (IGI), 1993 edition, it is wise to contact the Ancestral File submitter. (Include a stamped, addressed envelope. Remember, you want him to share with you his information and his time; don't expect him to pay the postage too.)

Abbreviations used in the LDS ordinance dates include: B for LDS baptism, E for temple endowment, SS for sealing to spouse, and SP for sealing to parents. See Special Helps for LDS on page 35.

5. *Merging Individual Detail.* When additional information was received in records submitted by someone else, it was added to the composite record for that person. Thus, if your record came in first, and contained only birth information, and mine came in later but also contained the christening information, the christening information would be added to the record, and my name would be added to the composite record as a submitter. However, if my submission contained birth or christening detail DIFFERENT from what was already listed in the record (but the records were still recognized as pertaining to the same person), your information already submitted would remain, the computer would simply drop my information for that item, but it would add my name as a submitter.

6. *Merging Linkages.* Sometimes individual records for some members of a family merged but records for other family members did not. These records often cause problems. For example, this has often resulted in matching and merging records of one or both parents, but not records of the children. Thus, thirteen children may be listed in a family that really had only eight children. Records of some of the children need to be merged. Also more than one parent may be shown because duplicate records for the same person need to be merged.

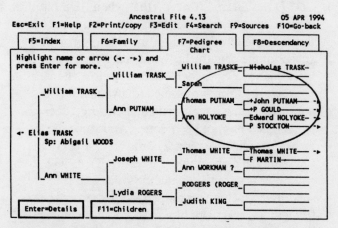

FIGURE 17 *Plus sign (+) on a pedigree chart means more than one record is linked to that person as a father or mother (Ancestral File)*

Example: If we extend the mother's pedigree shown in Figure 3, on the Trask line we would find a Thomas Putnam, with parents John Putnam and Priscilla. The pedigree chart shows a plus sign (+) beside the names of John and his wife.

If we press ENTER, we find other couples (a different record for one or both of the parents) listed in this position. By pressing the F12 key, the names and Ancestral File record numbers (AFN) for both will be shown.

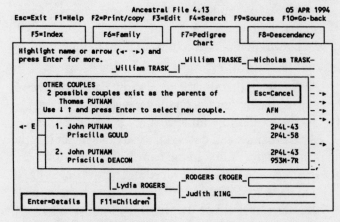

FIGURE 18 *The names and AFNs for the multiple parents are displayed by pressing F12 (Ancestral File)*

The appearance of the plus sign on the pedigree chart may mean the person has two lines that need to be shown. It is intended to reflect different persons, such as a bloodline and an adopted line, or where there are two different documented possibilities for parents. At present, however, it more often means that two or more records need to be merged.

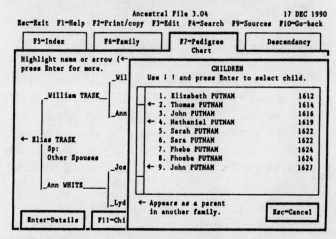

FIGURE 19 *Brief display of children linked to John Putnam and Priscilla Gould (Ancestral File)*

In Figure 18, we note that the father, John Putnam, has the same Ancestral File record number (AFN) in both sets of parents, so we know there is only one record listed for the father. But there are two possibilities for the mother. In the family group record, we find that the same children are given two mothers: Priscilla Gould and Priscilla Deacon. (While John may have been married to both women, both could not have been the mother of the same children. Research needs to be done to determine which is correct.) In rare cases one wife could be a natural mother to a child and a different wife could be an adopted or sealed mother to the same child. But that is the exception, and would certainly not be expected for this early time period.

Now, looking at the family of nine children for John Putnam and Priscilla Gould (see Figure 19), we notice that we have two named John, two named Sarah and two named Phebe. Consider carefully. Of course, it is possible to have more than one child by the same name. If one child died young, it was not unusual for another child to be given the same name. In this case, this may be true for the two Johns; one was born in 1616, one in 1627. More research is needed to determine if this represents records for two persons, or a duplicate record for the same person. For Sarah and Phebe, the problem is different. Both records for Sarah list the birth date as 1622, but one name is spelled Sara, the other Sarah. The computer considers these different names, but the detail shows exactly the same full birth or christening date for Sara and Sarah. With Phebe, the variant spelling of Phoebe is used for one record; otherwise the records are identical. It is obvious, then, that the records need to be merged.

Caution: Two records in the file for the same person that have not been merged can have significance to you as a file user. If you locate and look at the pedigree for each record, you may find additional generations that you may miss by looking at only one record for that person.

The two records for James Harvie, referred to earlier, are a good example. If you find only the record with his name listed as a husband to his wife and no information linking him to any parents or pedigree, you will think there is nothing in the file on his ancestors. But if you also find the record for him linked to his parents, you will find his grandparents, great-grandparents, etc. Without both records, part of the information contained in Ancestral File about this person, his ancestors, his spouse, and her ancestors will be missed. This type of duplication may be found by looking in the index and tracing each duplicate there, or sometimes by tracing the records of two or more mothers or fathers who are linked to a person but whose records need to be merged.

Take your pedigree chart and look in the Ancestral File index for each name, to see if more than one record is listed for that person. If so, and the name of a parent is displayed in the brief display, look at a pedigree chart for each record.

Ancestral File Number Changed

If you have an Ancestral File number (AFN) that you have obtained from an old printout, the computer may tell you it has been merged into another record and now has a different AFN.

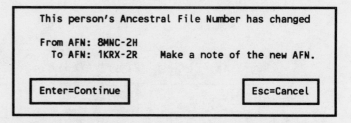

FIGURE 20 *AFN change notice (Ancestral File).*

Corrections

The first edition of Ancestral File did not allow corrections to the data. Now you can make some corrections to the data from any display, along with simple merges from the index or family group record.

1. *Preparation.*

   • Be sure to have all of the complete and correct details for all family members at your finger tips before you sit down to begin a correction session.

   • When you begin in the index, make several searches without going into more details for any of the persons. This will place the index entry in the GO BACK area, and you can then access all of these records by using the F10 key without having to return to the index disc each time. In this way, for example, you could view pedigree charts or family group records, see a list of submitters, or edit the records for James Harvie, Diantha Nichols, Eli Oliver, and others without needing to return to the index discs.

Records can also be accessed, of course, by going up and down a pedigree, if they are on the same pedigree. You may need to use family groups to go down the line, as well as the pedigree to go up the line.

2. *Overview.* The corrections process will follow a few simple steps:

• Find the record you wish to either change or add genealogical or LDS ordinance details to; or two records that you wish to merge in the index or in the same family group. (No changes can be made to records of living persons except to add a death date and place, or an LDS baptism date. [The place of baptism can go in the source documentation field.])

• Place the highlight bar on that name.

• Press the F3 key to edit the information.

• Follow the simple instructions given on the screen.

For example, if a field is blank, type in the correct information or type over the existing information. For merges, place the first record in the edit position by pressing ENTER. Move the cursor to the second entry, and press the space bar. You will then see both records individually and the merged record displayed on the screen. (See Figure 23.) The system will identify the differences in the records before it displays them for you. You can also edit the merged record if you desire. Pressing the F12 key will save your changes. You will be asked to give a reason and source information for each change.

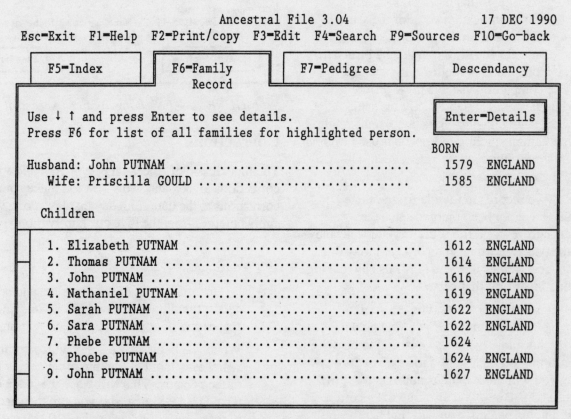

```
                        Ancestral File 3.04                    17 DEC 1990
        Esc-Exit  F1-Help  F2-Print/copy  F3-Edit  F4-Search  F9-Sources  F10-Go-back

        ┌─────────────────┐ ┌─────────────────┐ ┌─────────────────┐ ┌─────────────────┐
        │    F5-Index      │ │    F6-Family     │ │   F7-Pedigree    │ │   Descendancy    │
        │                  │ │     Record       │ │                  │ │                  │

           Use ↓ ↑ and press Enter to see details.          ┌─────────────────┐
           Press F6 for list of all families for highlighted│  Enter-Details  │
                                                             └─────────────────┘
                                                              BORN
           Husband: John PUTNAM .................................   1579   ENGLAND
              Wife: Priscilla GOULD ..............................   1585   ENGLAND


           Children

           ┌──────────────────────────────────────────────────────────────────────┐
              1. Elizabeth PUTNAM ................................   1612   ENGLAND
              2. Thomas PUTNAM ...................................   1614   ENGLAND
              3. John PUTNAM .....................................   1616   ENGLAND
              4. Nathaniel PUTNAM ................................   1619   ENGLAND
              5. Sarah PUTNAM ....................................   1622   ENGLAND
              6. Sara PUTNAM .....................................   1622   ENGLAND
              7. Phebe PUTNAM ....................................   1624
              8. Phoebe PUTNAM ...................................   1624   ENGLAND
              9. John PUTNAM .....................................   1627   ENGLAND
```

*FIGURE 21 Begin the process of merging records for two children by going
into the family group display (Ancestral File)*

This does not change the record on the compact disc. Changes you have made will be recorded on a diskette, which you will send to the Family History Department in Salt Lake City. It will be added to the master file, and will appear in a future edition of Ancestral File on compact disc.

For example, to merge the two records for Sarah listed in the John Putnam and Priscilla Gould family, we must be in the family group record display:

With the highlight bar on one of the names you wish to merge (in this case Sarah), press the F3 key, and the Edit menu will look like this:

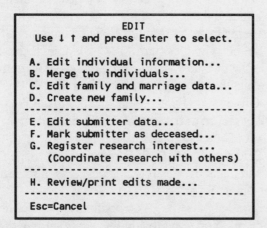

```
              EDIT
    Use ↓ ↑ and press Enter to select.

    A. Edit individual information...
    B. Merge two individuals...
    C. Edit family and marriage data...
    D. Create new family...
    -------------------------------------
    E. Edit submitter data...
    F. Mark submitter as deceased...
    G. Register research interest...
       (Coordinate research with others)
    -------------------------------------
    H. Review/print edits made...
    -------------------------------------
    Esc=Cancel
```

FIGURE 22 Edit menu is displayed by pressing F3 (Ancestral File)

You want to select option C (merge two individuals).

Instructions on the screen will tell you to insert a diskette, giving the address where to mail it when the correction process is complete. Write down the address, or see page 24 in this publication.

Next, the computer will ask you to identify the person requesting the correction. A screen with blanks for you to type in a name and address will appear. Corrections cannot be requested without the name and address of the requestor which should be listed the same way each time. The telephone number is optional.

Next, move the highlight bar to the second name to be merged into this record (in this case, Sara), and press the space bar.

A screen telling you the differences in the records will appear. In this case, it will tell you that the names are different. (**You** can tell it is the same person with variations in the spelling of the name, but to the computer it is a different name.) You need to use your own judgment.

The screen will then display three records—the two you have selected to merge, and the merged record. Press the F12 key to complete the merge.

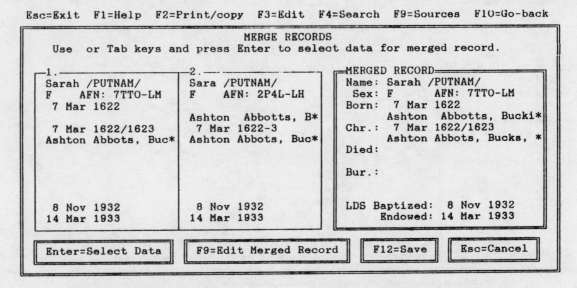

```
Esc=Exit   F1=Help   F2=Print/copy   F3=Edit   F4=Search   F9=Sources   F10=Go-back
┌─────────────────────────────────────────────────────────────────────────────┐
│                           MERGE RECORDS                                       │
│        Use   or Tab keys and press Enter to select data for merged record.    │
│                                                                               │
│ ┌1.──────────────┐ ┌2.──────────────┐ ┌MERGED RECORD───────────────┐          │
│ │Sarah /PUTNAM/  │ │Sara /PUTNAM/   │ │Name: Sarah /PUTNAM/        │          │
│ │F     AFN: 7TTO-LM│ │F    AFN: 2P4L-LH│ │ Sex: F       AFN: 7TTO-LM │          │
│ │7 Mar 1622      │ │                │ │Born:   7 Mar 1622          │          │
│ │                │ │Ashton  Abbotts, B*│ │      Ashton  Abbotts, Bucki*│        │
│ │7 Mar 1622/1623 │ │7 Mar 1622-3    │ │Chr.:  7 Mar 1622/1623      │          │
│ │Ashton Abbots, Buc*│ │Ashton Abbots, Buc*│ │      Ashton Abbots, Bucks, *│     │
│ │                │ │                │ │Died:                       │          │
│ │                │ │                │ │                            │          │
│ │                │ │                │ │Bur.:                       │          │
│ │                │ │                │ │                            │          │
│ │8 Nov 1932      │ │8 Nov 1932      │ │LDS Baptized:  8 Nov 1932   │          │
│ │14 Mar 1933     │ │14 Mar 1933     │ │     Endowed: 14 Mar 1933   │          │
│ └────────────────┘ └────────────────┘ └────────────────────────────┘          │
│  ┌──────────────────┐ ┌─────────────────────┐ ┌──────────┐ ┌──────────┐       │
│  │ Enter=Select Data│ │ F9=Edit Merged Record│ │ F12=Save │ │Esc=Cancel│       │
│  └──────────────────┘ └─────────────────────┘ └──────────┘ └──────────┘       │
└─────────────────────────────────────────────────────────────────────────────┘
```

FIGURE 23 The merging process displays three records (Ancestral File)

You will be required to give the reason/sources for your request to merge these records. This is your chance to give documentation and brief evidence to support your request.

When you have finished the editing process, the record on the screen will not reflect the change. The change is recorded on the diskette that must be sent to Salt Lake City. You will receive a printed report showing the records before and after the changes.

3. Additional Corrections and Edits.

To merge two or more records into one, merge each one separately into the same primary record. In our example, if you found in the index yet another record for Sarah Putnam, you would also merge it into the record for her that has the AFN 7TT0-LM (and if you had three others, you would merge them each one individually into this same primary record). Therefore, it is important that you keep track of which record you use as the primary one. You can do this by either writing down the AFN or by making a screen print of the merge process. (You may find additional records that need to be merged into the one by looking for her name in the index.) All of these merges will come into the same record when the information on the floppy diskette is added to Ancestral File in Salt Lake City.

Linking generations when descendants and ancestors are in Ancestral File but one generation is missing can be done by using the correction process. Follow these steps:

- Find the record of the descendant who is in the file, but whose parent is not.

- With the highlight on this name, press the F3 (edit) key. The Edit Menu (see Figure 22) will appear on the screen.

For example, we have found the record of Charles Fremont Oliver in Ancestral File, with some of his descendants. His parents have been name-only records in the first edition (see page 14), and now are there with only estimated dates. His father is Eli Noyes Oliver and his mother is Diantha Hannah Nichols, daughter of John Nichols who was born 1784 in Maine. (Listed in the index with father George Nichols.) We want to fill in the exact dates and places for the records of Eli Noyes Oliver and Diantha Hannah Nichols, link Diantha's record to her parents' records, and create records for Eli's father and mother.

- Select option D (Edit Family and Marriage Data), and make the desired changes to each record. (Diantha was born 2 Oct 1832 in Starks, Somerset, Maine. You could also add her death detail. You want to add this along with her LDS ordinance dates. See Figure 24.)

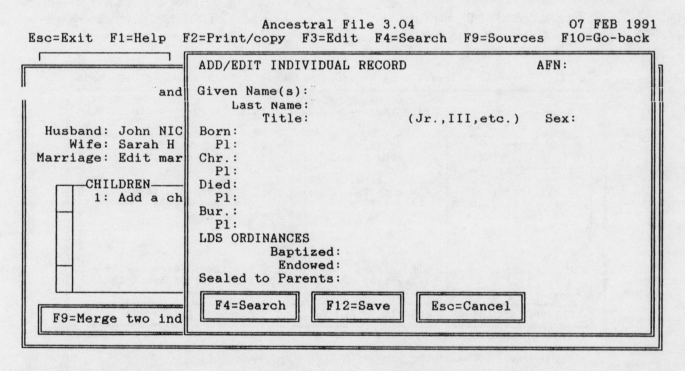

FIGURE 24 *This screen allows you to add or correct information to an existing record or create a record not previously in the file (Ancestral File)*

- Proofread your information carefully, and press the F12 key to save your information. It is stored on the diskette that will later be sent to Salt Lake City.

- You may want to also make a screen print of this record, although you will later be able to make a

printout of all the changes and additions made during your work session.

- Now you want to link Diantha also to the record of her parents, John Nichols and Sarah Skillings. To do this, simply add her record to their family, being careful to use the same name, dates, and places used in the record where she is listed as a wife and mother. (See Figure 24.) When the records are added to Ancestral File, they will merge, which will link the generations together.

To do this, again select option D (Edit Family and Marriage Data). Move the cursor to the child position, and add the genealogical information for Diantha. (This is creating a totally separate record, but when the records merge in Ancestral File, this will link Diantha to both her ancestors and her descendants.)

Note. You do not remove a record if it can possibly be merged into another record.

Sometimes a record for a child linked into the family does not belong and cannot be merged into another child's record. For example, one person found that her grandmother was listed with 23 children. But when a study of the children's records was made, nine of them really belonged to another family and were not duplicates of records for the other children. These children would need to be removed from the family. This does not often happen, but it sometimes does.

```
                    Ancestral File 4.13              05 APR 1994
Esc=Exit  F1=Help  F2=Print/copy  F3=Edit  F4=Search  F9=Sources  F10=Go-back
┌──────┐ ┌──────┐ ┌──────┐ ┌──────┐
│                          EDIT FAMILY
│        Use ↓ ↑ and press Enter to select item or individual to edit.
│                                                        Born/Chr.
│ Husband: John NICHOLS .........................  14 Jun 1784
│    Wife: Sarah H SKILLINGS .....................  1790
│ Marriage: Edit marriage data (and LDS sealing to spouse)
│  ┌─CHILDREN────────────────────────────────────┐
│  │ 1: Add a child                               │
│  │                                              │
│  │                                              │
│  │                                              │
│  └──────────────────────────────────────────────┘
│ ┌──────────────────┐ ┌──────────────┐ ┌──────────┐ ┌────────────┐
│ │F9=Merge two individuals│ │Delete=Remove│ │F12=Save│ │Esc=Cancel│
│ └──────────────────┘ └──────────────┘ └──────────┘ └────────────┘
```

FIGURE 25 Select C *from the edit menu and this screen will appear, allowing you to add/correct details on any family member, merge records for two children listed, remove a child whose record cannot be merged into another but who does not belong to this family, or add the record of a child not previously in the file (Ancestral File)*

- It is possible to add other children's records to the family also, following the same procedure. But usually you will want to add them just as regular additional records in a submission to the file.

- If you want to also add the names of parents for Eli Noyes Oliver, husband to Diantha Nichols, you must first be in the family group record where Eli is listed as a parent, and then press the F3 key. Select option D (Create new family). When it asks whether you wish to create a new family as a parent or as a child (see Figure 27), select child. The spaces for you to fill in the information on his father and mother will then be displayed. (See Figure 24). After you have typed in the information, press the F12 key to save it.

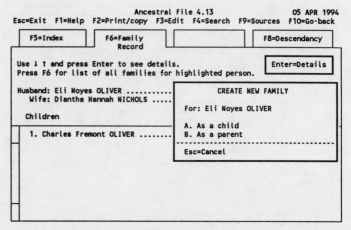

FIGURE 26 Select D to create a new family, and choose whether the person will be a child or a parent (Ancestral File)

- If you want to add the place of marriage for a record already in the file, first go to the family group record for that person. Then press the F3 (edit) key. Select C (Edit family and marriage data). You will be able to add the place of marriage. If you also wish to add the LDS date of temple sealing, you can do this at the same time. (See Figure 28, which shows an aunt to John Nichols, Mary Nichols and her husband Uriah Weatherbee.) Remember that when the names were submitted on the old style family group record, there was no space to put the place of marriage or the LDS sealing to spouse when the person was listed as a child on the form. Therefore, there are many of these records that need to have the additional detail added. Complete the process by following the regular procedures of pressing the F12 key to save the record, and providing the source of your information.

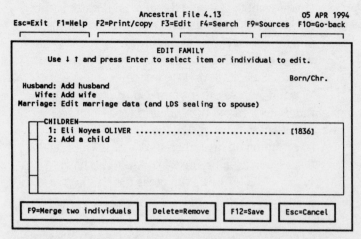

FIGURE 27 *When you select the role of child, you can add records for the father (husband), mother (wife), and other children (Ancestral File)*

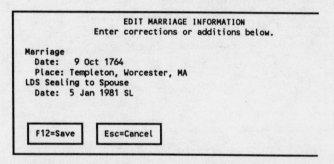

FIGURE 28 *Edit Marriage Information allows adding marriage date, place or LDS temple sealing date (Ancestral File)*

4. **Report of Corrections.** When you have completed your session, you can make a printed report of the changes you have made. Since these changes will not show until the next edition of Ancestral File on compact disc, it is important that you preserve the record of the changes you have made so you will not submit them more than once.

5. *Avoiding Problems.* There is a great need to be correct in the first place.

   • Typing errors may cause duplication. For example, a submission contained a misspelling of the name Joseph as Jaseph. When records of more than one submitter were merged, this made two children in the family with the same identity, one spelled JAseph, one JOseph. The records were merged and corrected manually by the staff, then the same submitter who submitted it the first time made another submission containing the same family with the same spelling error. The

family again has an extra child, with his name spelled JAseph, which must be hand-merged into the record of the JOseph spelling.

   • A family may have the right number of children in the 1989 edition of Ancestral File, but if another submission comes in, with slightly different dates and/or names for the children, the parents' records may merge but some of the children would not. The 1990 edition, therefore, may show twenty-one children for the family.

   • Use of the word UNKNOWN will also cause records to fail to merge. Unless you have dates or places that need to be added, it is better to leave the name space blank. The Personal Ancestral File software will allow the selection of UNKNOWN when entering the data, but will not insert the word in the record.

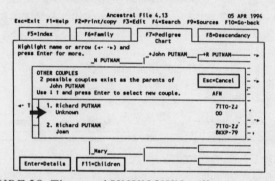

FIGURE 29 *The word UNKNOWN will not merge with a name (Ancestral File)*

   • There is also a need to avoid placing the term MRS in the title field, if it is used with the husband's first given name. For example, you may have a death date for the wife, but do not know her name. You may create a record for her as Mrs. Edward Hilton. The Personal Ancestral File has a field labeled TITLE, where the term **Mrs.** is often placed. But when Personal Ancestral File records are loaded into Ancestral File, the title field is discarded (because so many different types of details have been recorded there by different submitters). Therefore you now have Edward Hilton married to Edward Hilton. (This can be avoided by placing the term MRS in the given name field, when needed.)

Be patient with other submitters and with the system. The Ancestral File is still in its infancy. Procedures are still developing, and, over time, solutions will be found for many of these problems.

You and others who care are needed to help work them out.

This new technique will undoubtedly need some smoothing out over time, but it is a wonderful beginning. It will allow everyone who wishes to do so to help in correcting and completing information in Ancestral File.

Sources

The only source in the 1992 edition is the name and address of each submitter. Some records have as many as 100 submitters, others have only one. To see how many·and who submitted the records that were merged into the existing record, press the F9 key. You will be asked to insert another disc. First you will be told how many submitters there are, and then the list of submitters and their addresses and submission number(s) will be displayed. Use the down-arrow key to scroll the screen to see all of them. (When the tiny arrow is displayed on the screen, it means there is additional information that you can see by scrolling the screen, using the up or down-arrow key.) You can view the list of submitters for any name on any of the pedigree charts or family group records you have just viewed, without needing to return to the index discs. (Use your GO BACK feature by pressing F10, and move to any chart listed there and press ENTER.) The computer has retained these displays in its memory, and does not need to again retrieve them from disc.

1. *Source Documentation.* It is anticipated that more source detail eventually will be included as part of Ancestral File on compact disc. Meantime, the source notes given with the corrections will become part of the history recorded in the individual record for each person. The individual record will also show how the entry read before the new information was added.

   If the submission was made earlier than 1989, there is a microfilm number beside the submitter's name. This refers to a microfilm copy of the pedigree chart and family group records submitted, where source references may be cited. Those submitted after 1989 are on diskette, and there is no microfilm copy of the information. (The disc is being stored, and source references listed eventually will be made available.)

2. *No Submitter Name.* Occasionally you may find a record with no submitter listed. This record was added manually by the Ancestral File Unit staff, at someone's request, before sources for corrections and additions began to be recorded, or was a name-only entry.

```
┌─────────────────────────────────────────┐
│              SOURCES                      │
│  Use ↓ ↑ and press Enter to select.       │
│                                           │
│  A. Submitters...                         │
│  B. Research interest...                  │
│  C. Family organizations...               │
│  D. Notes and history of changes...       │
│  ---------------------------------------  │
│  Esc=Cancel                               │
└─────────────────────────────────────────┘
```

FIGURE 30 Sources Menu (Ancestral File)

3. *Research Interest.* The ability to register or display research interest indicators is not included in the first edition of Ancestral File, but it will be in a future release. Press the HELP key (F1) for more information when it becomes available.

   The principle of registering a research interest is that you have something to give: either you are doing active research on that name and wish to coordinate with others, or you have previously done research on the name and are willing to share what you have. There will be a limit on the number of research interest flags that one person can set. All those who register a research interest must be willing to answer ALL correspondence (as long as a stamp is included), and must agree to keep their own address current in the file. Research interest indicators in Ancestral File will eventually replace the Family Registry, which is now available on microfiche.

   When registration begins, you will be able to register by calling up your name as a submitter and indicating your wish to have a research interest registered for a specific name. This will be done from the Sources menu.

4. *Family Organizations.* The 1989 release of Ancestral File does not allow for registering family organizations. In a future release you will be able to register a family organization's interest in a name already in the file. Eventually the file will include both ancestral and surname organizations.

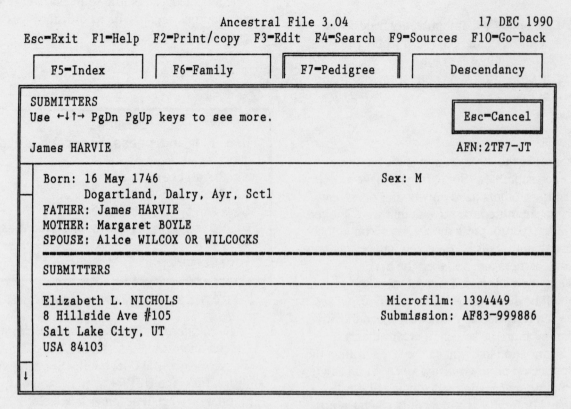

FIGURE 31 Submitter name and address (Ancestral File)

Contributing Your Researched Family Information to Ancestral File

The way to make the file more useful to everyone is to make it more complete and more perfect. Your contribution is important.

1. *How to Prepare your Contribution*

   • If possible, see what is already in the file, since part or all of your ancestry may already be there. Build on what is there, helping to perfect, correct and complete it, rather than submitting another record that may not merge correctly with the existing records.

   • Type your information into a computer, using a genealogy software program that includes GEDCOM (see glossary, page 49). The Personal Ancestral File is one of these programs, and has a special function just to help you download records from a family records directory (file) to submit to the Ancestral File.

   • Send the diskette **in GEDCOM format** to the Ancestral File Operations Unit, 50 East North

Temple Street, Salt Lake City, Utah 84150.

(Please note: It must be in GEDCOM format.)

That is all there is to it, and there is no charge.

If you don't have a computer, ask around in your community, and see what is available. Many family history centers, genealogical societies, and individuals have computers with the Personal Ancestral File genealogy software, and may allow you to enter it or have it entered for you.

The information submitted will be held until another compact disk is made, will be added to the master data base, and included in the next edition of Ancestral File.

2. *Personal Ancestral File Provides Special Helps.* To create an Ancestral File submission from your Personal Ancestral File (**version MS DOS 2.2 or 2.3**) follow these simple steps:

   • From the access menu, select 2 (Genealogical Information Exchange).

```
------------------------
PERSONAL ANCESTRAL FILE
------------------------
Release 2.3 (22 Nov 1993)

        ACCESS MENU

1. Family Records
2. Genealogical Information Exchange
3. Research Data Filer
4. Family Records Check
5. Family Records Check/Repair
6. Configure Programs
0. Return to System


    Please enter your selection:
```

FIGURE 32 Access Menu (Personal Ancestral File, 2.3)

- When the next screen appears, select option 1 (Ancestral File Submission)

- The next screen displays the name of your default family records directory (file). If that is where your records are stored that you want to submit, then accept that by pressing ENTER. (See Figure 33.)
But if you have more than one family records file (directory), and this is not the one you want to submit from, type over the information in line two, to conform to your path to the data. (Some people have it as shown, C:\paf\NICHOLS; while others may have it just C:\data\, or C:\Nichols. If you do not have a hard disk, then you would type over it with an A followed by a colon [A:].)

```
                    ------------------------
                    ANCESTRAL FILE SUBMISSION
                    ------------------------



Today's Date (DD MMM YYYY):  31 Jan 1991

Family Records Data Disk:  C:\PAF\NICHOLS\  <--

        Submission Disk:  A:  <--

File Name For Submission:  NICHOL
```

FIGURE 33 Shows the directory (file) that your records will be taken from (change it when needed) (Personal Ancestral File, 2.3)

- A subsequent menu will ask you if you want your submission to be for the ancestors of the person selected, or for his descendants. (Usually, it is suggested that you make an ancestral submission.)

```
-------------------------------
ANCESTRAL FILE SUBMISSION MENU
-------------------------------

What type of submission do you want to create?

            1. ANCESTOR Submission
            2. DESCENDANT Submission
            3. FAMILY Submission
            4. All Records
            0. Return to Main Menu

    Please enter your selection:
```

FIGURE 34 Usually you will select A, ancestor submission (Personal Ancestral File, 2.3)

- If you have selected ancestral submission (option 1), the next screen will ask you to select the beginning individual. You can do this by typing in the record identification number (RIN), or by typing in selected information onto a request screen, and allowing the computer to retrieve the record for you to review. Either way, you will have the chance to look at the record to verify that it is for the person you want to begin with.

```
-------------------------------------
ANCESTRAL FILE SUBMISSION--ANCESTOR
-------------------------------------

        SELECT BEGINNING INDIVIDUAL

1. Know RIN
2. Do not know RIN
0. Return to Ancestral File Submission Menu

        Please enter your selection:
```

FIGURE 35 Identify the person whose pedigree you want to download (Personal Ancestral File, 2.3)

- The next screen will allow you to tell the computer how many generations you want transferred. Perhaps you want 9 generations. (Maximum is 50.) Type in the number.

Note: In selecting the person to be listed as number 1, you need to understand that this will automatically include that person's brothers and sisters and the children of that person and his or her brothers and sisters. If you have not obtained permission to submit all these records to Ancestral File, and they are living persons, you may want to select a different person as no. 1. For example, you may begin with each of your four grandparents, and make four different submissions on the same diskette.

- The computer will retrieve the records requested, and evaluate them. It will give brief comments on those with incomplete information. For example:

```
ANCESTRAL FILE SUBMISSION              BORN/CHR.      PAR-RIN  SP-RIN
-----------------------------------------------------------------------------
Bethia MEACHAM-36                        1650           32           OK
Rebecca MEACHAM-37                       1655           32           OK
Alice DOUCH-38                                                   32   OK
Henry TRASK-39                           1625                    40   OK
Mary SOUTHWICK-40            Abt         1628           77       39   See comments
Sarah TRASK-41                                          39            See comments
John BROWNE-42              11 Oct       1601           79       43   OK
Dorothy KENT-43                          1603                    42   OK

=============================================================================
                              COMMENTS
If you can provide        If you can provide
the individual's birth    the individual's birth
or christening DATE,      or christening PLACE,
it will help prevent      it will help prevent
duplicated records in     duplicated records in
the Ancestral File.       the Ancestral File.

F1 CONTINUE      F2 QUIT       F3 PRINT       F4 EDIT            ARROW KEYS MORE
```

FIGURE 36 Comments on records selected to submit to Ancestral File help
identify problems (Personal Ancestral File, 2.2)

- The computer will download only notes that are "tagged". This means they have an explanation (!) in front of the note, as !Vital records of Greene, Androscoggin, Maine. This allows you to have biographical notes in your file that are not appropriate to send with your Ancestral File submission.

- The next screen will provide a place for you to type in your name and address, as the submitter of the records. The telephone number is optional.

- If you have more records than will go on one diskette, the computer will prompt you to insert another:
  Should you need a third disk, it would again prompt you. Notice that each ending is different. The first one is NICHOLS00.GED, the second ends with GOO, and the third would end with GO1.

- The computer will next tell you that it is processing the records, and then how many individual and marriage records were included.

- The computer will ask you (in a question at the bottom of the screen) if you want to make another Ancestral File submission. You will type Y for yes or N for no.

```
Please replace the AF Submission disk in:
   A:

with a formatted disk to contain the continuation file:
   NICHOL00.GOO
```

FIGURE 37 Computer prompts when more than one
diskette is needed in the download (Personal Ancestral
File, 2.2)

- The next screen will tell you how to label and mail your diskettes, and the address of where to mail them. It will ask if you want help in doing this. If you say yes, then it automatically prints out the form for you to submit with the diskettes. There is a place for you to type any note that you wish to have accompany your submission.

• The computer will then ask you if you want a printed report of your submission. (It is a good idea to say yes, but is a personal choice.)

The computer will then return to the previous menu, and you can exit the system by following the instruction on the screen.

INTERNATIONAL GENEALOGICAL INDEX

The International Genealogical Index (IGI) is the oldest computer data base at the Family History Department. The data base began in 1961. It has been available extensively on microfiche since 1973; the 1992 edition is available only on microfiche; the 1993 edition only on computer. It began to be available on compact disc in 1988. No modem access presently exists.

The 1993 edition is the most current one available (as of 3-94), and contains more than 200 million names of deceased persons. These records are not linked into family groups or pedigree charts. Even though entries may include the names of parents or a spouse, there is no link that ties the record of a person's birth to the record of his marriage, if both are in the file. And even though his parents' records of birth and/or marriage may be in the file, there will be no link between the child's record and that of his or her parents.

Uses

The International Genealogical Index indexes millions of different records from thousands of sources. It may enable you to:

1. *Find an extract of records* about your deceased ancestors. It contains millions of births, christening, and marriages and some miscellaneous sources such as probate records and partial census records for the United States and Canada. (There are NO records of living persons in the International Genealogical Index.)

2. *Identify possible pedigree connections* to extend your pedigree.

3. *Avoid duplicating* what has already been done.

4. *Trace most entries* to the source of input into the computer (by using the batch number). You can then evaluate the record in that setting, and perhaps find other helpful information.

5. *For LDS Church members*, determine the dates for sacred temple ordinances. (The International Genealogical Index does not presently index all temple ordinances for the deceased. When the Family Record Extraction program entries from all temple records performed prior to 1970 are added, it will be complete to the date of cut-off for each edition. The records for ordinances done 1978-1990 with "incomplete" birth or marriage detail have already been added. Some of the pre-1970 proxy baptism and proxy baptism & endowment records have been added. The others will be added, along with sealings of couples and sealings of child to parents. *Until this is done, the IGI remains only a partial index to temple work*.) See page 35 for more information for LDS members.

While it is published to help members of the LDS Church avoid duplication in their family history work, it is made available to anyone to use in personal research.

Record Elements

The amount of information contained in a record is limited to:

1. *Name* (of principal, and often of one or both parents for birth or christening records, or of spouse in marriage records). When no name of parent or spouse is included in the temple record for pre-1970 entries, the name of a Relative (REL) may be listed. This was the first male (or other early convert) of that family to join the LDS Church, and could be living or dead when the record was submitted.

2. *Sex Code*

3. *Event Type* (B for birth, C for christening, M for marriage, N for census [limited to a few partial census records for U.S and Canada], W for will, and S for miscellaneous, with a very few D for death date, and F for a substitute marriage record

4. *Event Date*

5. *Event Place* (usually at least county and state or country)

6. *LDS Church Ordinance Dates* (have limited significance in research); and

7. *Batch Number* (a reference number that can be traced to the source of input), with sheet number for some entries. The microfilm number of the input source and an explanation of the type of source used for that entry is also listed. (Many entries now have no batch numbers.)

Begin in the Right Locality

Localities are divided into large geographical areas, such as the United States and Canada (listed as North America), the British Isles, Germany, Norway, etc. A menu will appear for you to select the region where your ancestor was born or married. (See Figure 38.) If you do not know the region, press the function key F11 to see a list of countries and their regions.

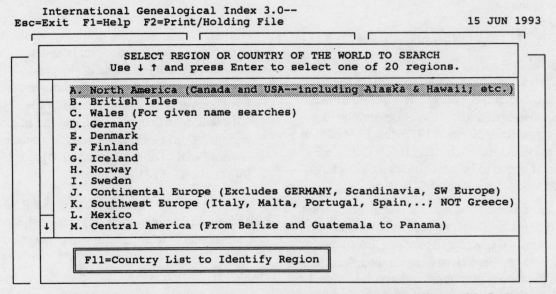

```
                International Genealogical Index 3.0--
       Esc=Exit  F1=Help  F2=Print/Holding File                     15 JUN 1993


                 SELECT REGION OR COUNTRY OF THE WORLD TO SEARCH
                  Use ↓ ↑ and press Enter to select one of 20 regions.

             A. North America (Canada and USA--including Alaska & Hawaii; etc.)
             B. British Isles
             C. Wales (For given name searches)
             D. Germany
             E. Denmark
             F. Finland
             G. Iceland
             H. Norway
             I. Sweden
             J. Continental Europe (Excludes GERMANY, Scandinavia, SW Europe)
             K. Southwest Europe (Italy, Malta, Portugal, Spain,..; NOT Greece)
             L. Mexico
          ↓  M. Central America (From Belize and Guatemala to Panama)


                 F11=Country List to Identify Region
```

FIGURE 38 Menu of geographical regions (International Genealogical Index)

Display

There are three types of displays to choose from (see figure 39).

Choose from the search menu the type of search you want to make. Usually you will begin with A, and later use B and C. You can move from one to the other by pressing a function key: F6 for Individual Search, F7 for Marriage Search, F8 for Parent Search.

1. *Individual Index, and Marriage Index*. These indexes are similar to the one for Ancestral File, displaying the names alphabetically by

   - Surname (you can choose to see the names by similar spelling or limited to exact spelling--see filters)

   - Given name (also grouped by a standard spelling)

   - Date of event (such as, birth, christening, father's probate, etc. in the Individual Index; by the marriage in Marriage Index)

- Middle names and initials are ignored. This is new in the 1993 edition, and is different from Ancestral File. (There is no way to retrieve a person by his/her middle name, such as Governor William Bradford whose record will appear as George William Bradford. You must know to look under George.)

- Date of the event within each name combination.

Caution: the International Genealogical Index has one big difference from Ancestral File: it is divided into major geographical regions. If you want to look for a record of a person who was born or married in the United States or Canada, you would select the North America region from the first menu. If you want to look at a record for a person born or married in England, or Germany, you would select the appropriate different region. (If a person was born in one region and married in another, you will need to look in both regions to find the two records.) To change regions, press the function key F11, and then move the highlight bar to the desired region and press ENTER.

```
┌──────────────────────────────────────────────────────────────────────┐
│                       SURNAME  SEARCH  MENU                            │
│          Use ↓ ↑ and press Enter to select a search.                   │
│     Similar surnames (last names) are intermixed in the search results.│
│                                                                        │
│   A. Individual Search (Birth/Christening information, etc.)           │
│   B. Marriage Search                                                   │
│   C. Parent Search (Individual index sorted by parent's names)         │
│      (You may find children grouped together by parents in this index.)│
│   ----------------------------------------------------------------------│
│      Esc=Cancel                                                        │
└──────────────────────────────────────────────────────────────────────┘
```

FIGURE 39 Search Menu (International Genealogical Index)

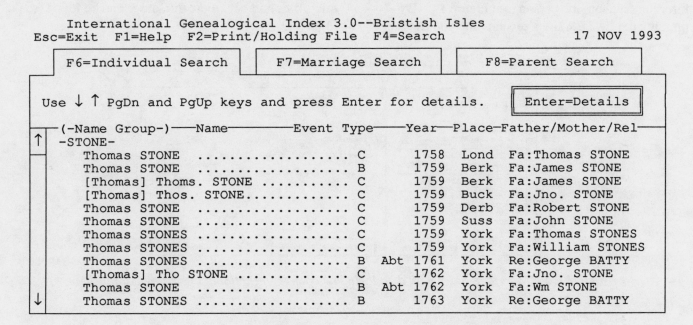

```
        International Genealogical Index 3.0--Bristish Isles
     Esc=Exit  F1=Help  F2=Print/Holding File  F4=Search        17 NOV 1993

       ┌─F6=Individual Search─┐   ┌─F7=Marriage Search─┐   ┌─F8=Parent Search─┐

      Use ↓ ↑ PgDn and PgUp keys and press Enter for details.    ┌Enter=Details┐

      ┌(-Name Group-)────Name────────Event Type────Year─Place─Father/Mother/Rel─
   ↑  -STONE-
           Thomas STONE   .................... C    1758  Lond  Fa:Thomas STONE
           Thomas STONE   .................... B    1759  Berk  Fa:James STONE
           [Thomas] Thoms. STONE ........... C    1759  Berk  Fa:James STONE
           [Thomas] Thos. STONE............. C    1759  Buck  Fa:Jno. STONE
           Thomas STONE   .................... C    1759  Derb  Fa:Robert STONE
           Thomas STONE   .................... C    1759  Suss  Fa:John STONE
           Thomas STONES .................... C    1759  York  Fa:Thomas STONES
           Thomas STONES .................... C    1759  York  Fa:William STONES
           Thomas STONES .................... B Abt 1761  York  Re:George BATTY
           [Thomas] Tho STONE ............. C    1762  York  Fa:Jno. STONE
           Thomas STONE   .................... B Abt 1762  York  Fa:Wm STONE
   ↓       Thomas STONES .................... B    1763  York  Re:George BATTY
```

FIGURE 40 Individual Index (International Genealogical Index)

The use of function keys to move from one type of
search to another is new with the 1993 edition of the
International Genealogical Index.

1994 Addendum (IGI)

The 1994 edition of the IGI is different from previous editions. It is a separate set of CD ROM discs, containing over 40 million names.

[1] Begin a search in the main file (1993 edition); [2] return to your request screen by pressing F6, F7, or F8; [3] choose B (modify request); [4] press F9 to change to the Addendum to access these additional records; [5] insert the requested disc (unless you are on a network); and press F12 to begin the search. (F9 will change to or from the Addendum.)

```
┌──────────────────────────────────────────┐
│  Current File:  Main IGI   1994 Addendum  │
│                                            │
│           F9=Change File                   │
└──────────────────────────────────────────┘
```

```
┌──────────────────────────────────────────┐
│    FROM INDIVIDUAL TO MARRIAGE SEARCH      │
│                                            │
│  Use ↓ ↑ and press Enter to select an option.│
│  A. (Individual) Thomas STONES             │
│  B. (Parents) William STONES/              │
│  C. New Marriage Search                    │
│  ------------------------------------------│
│  Esc=Cancel                                │
└──────────────────────────────────────────┘
```

*FIGURE 40A Press the F7 function key to move to the
Marriage Index. It will retain the information from the
previous search, which you can accept or alter.*

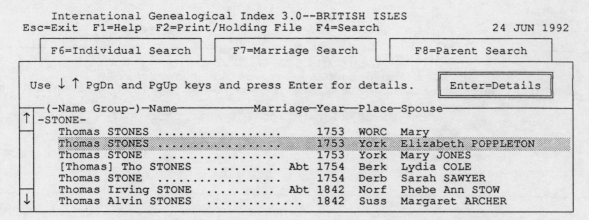

FIGURE 40B Marriage Index (International Genealogical Index)

By pressing the ENTER key you can see more detailed information about the person (see Figure 41). By pressing the ENTER key a second time you can see information about the source of the entry, and the microfilm number where the source can be found (see Figure 42).

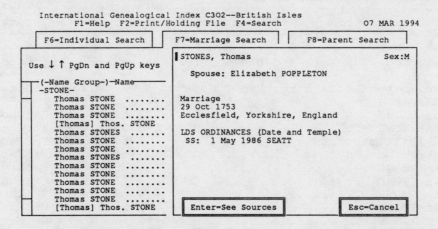

FIGURE 41 Marriage Index with detail window open (International Genealogical Index)

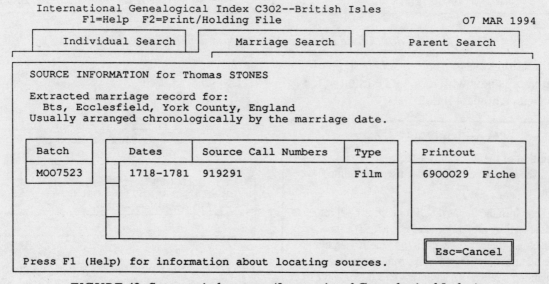

FIGURE 42 Source window open (International Genealogical Index)

2. *Parent Index.* The parent index displays the entries for the child or children alphabetically by the name(s) of the parent or parents.

This may bring together several or all of the children of a parent or couple, plus often many others who had parent(s) by the same name(s). Pressing ENTER while in the Parent Index will display details for the child. To find details on the parent(s) you must find their records in the index. (A person may be listed as a parent in the index and not be listed there as an individual.)

```
┌────────────────────────────────────────────────┐
│        FROM MARRIAGE TO PARENT SEARCH            │
│                                                  │
│  Use ↓ ↑ and press Enter to select an option.    │
│                                                  │
│  A. (Parents) Thomas STONES/Elizabeth POPPLETON  │
│  B. New Parent Search                            │
│  ----------------------------------------------- │
│  Esc=Cancel                                      │
└────────────────────────────────────────────────┘
```

FIGURE 42A Press F8 to move to the Parent Index

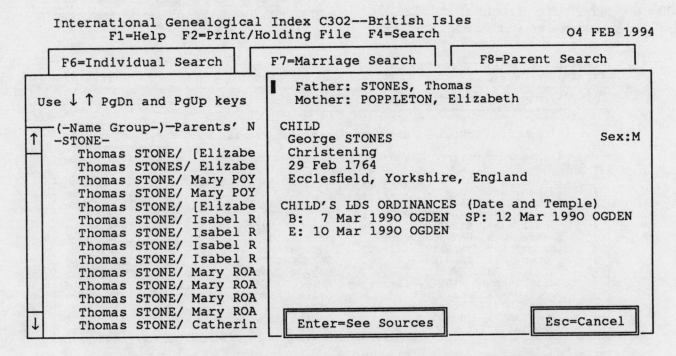

```
International Genealogical Index C302--British Isles
        F1=Help  F2=Print/Holding File  F4=Search        04 FEB 1994
```

FIGURE 43 *Parent Index with window open also displays details only on the child*
(International Genealogical Index)

The secret to finding children using the Parent Index is to know how the parents' names are listed in the entries for the various children. Sometimes they are all listed the same, but often they are not. You can find this by guessing, or by looking in the Individual Index for the record of a child, and see how the names of the parents are listed. Then with the highlight on that entry, press the F8 key and then F12, and see how many of the children's records are retrieved.

For example, you may look for the record for Martha Harvie, born about 1811 in Hants County, Nova Scotia, Canada, daughter of James and Martha Harvie, and wife of Isaac Sanford. Look in the index for Martha,

and browse the listings. If there are too many, limit the entries displayed to only those from Nova Scotia by pressing the F10 key and filtering (see page 33) the records. Note a record for Martha, daughter of James, that comes from a probate record of 1834, with the right locality. The father's name is listed as JAS. HARVIE, and there is no mother's name listed.

Go to the parent index by pressing F8, and again press the F10 key to filter (select your locality by highlighting it and pressing ENTER, and then press the F12 key). The records for Martha and her brothers and sisters are displayed in the right-hand portion of the screen. (Details are not given for the parents.)

In this example note that the standard spelling of given names retrieves JAS with JAMES.

This is not a typical entry. The records are from a probate record, which is unusual. You would not have recognized the entry for the child unless you were alert. And you may not have noticed it if you had not filtered down to look at only the records from Nova Scotia, to make the listing small enough to look at a variety of years. While the percentage of records in the file that are probate records is not great, there are enough of them, especially for the United States and Canada, to make it worth your effort to watch for them. Probate records, along with partial census records for the United States and Canada, were accepted from 1969-1978.

Often the mother's name is not listed, and when it is included it does not always list the maiden surname.

For example, if you are interested in Mary Woodcock, born in 1830 in Yorkshire, England, begin by finding her record in the Individual Index and note that her parents are listed as William Woodcock and Hannah Stones. Try this in the Parent Index, and you will find no other children. Next look in the Individual Index for a sister, Encora Woodcock, and find that her record lists the parents as William Woodcock and Hannah. Use this in the Parent Index and limit the records to children born or christened in Yorkshire, England. You will find records of several of her brothers and sisters in this way. (It is helpful to note the parish where each child is born, but it is not possible to filter to the parish level in the International Genealogical Index. However, in Personal Ancestral File, after you have uploaded your GEDCOM file, it is possible to do searches and printouts on the parish level.)

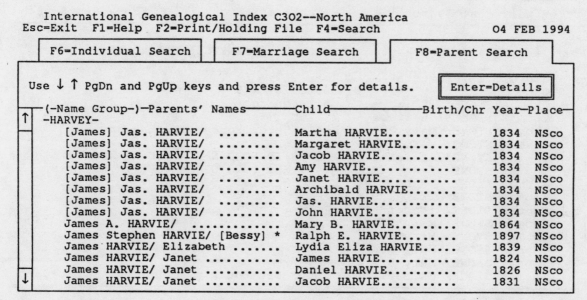

FIGURE 44 *Parent Index lists names of parent or parents on one side and names of children on the other (International Genealogical Index)*

You might next look just under William Woodcock (with no mother's name listed), again filtering to include only records of children born in Yorkshire. You may also look under the name of the mother.

Hint: You can further do your "homework" on this by looking in the microfiche edition of the International Genealogical Index and seeing how the parents' names are listed for families you particularly want to download (copy) the records for.

Sometimes the name of neither parent is included, even though the child's record is listed in the index. These names must be found through use of the Individual Index. For example, there may still be one record you

want. The baptism for Mary's sister Encora Woodcock was done by proxy in this extracted record. You know that she was a member of the LDS Church in life, and was already married when she joined. Her name may have been included in the extraction of the early LDS branch and ward records, but she may be listed in the index under her married surname. You now go back to the Individual Index, and look for Encora Batty (her married surname), and find an additional record for her under that name. (The two records for Mary--the one extracted from her baptism record into the LDS Church in 1853 and the one where she was christened as a child into another church--were not considered duplicates because the identifying information did not match. If an entry for a person already exists, with the same basic identifiers so that it matches, the extraction entry is not added.)

Marriage records are not included in the Parent Index, because names of parents are not included in the IGI marriage entry.

Special Features

1. *Filtering.* You can narrow your search by use of the FILTERING function. For example, you have all of the records for the United States and Canada in one listing. If you would like to limit the ones retrieved to one or more states, such as Maine and New Hampshire, you can select the filtering function (press the F10 key, rather than F12) and select the locality filter, then mark your localities by pressing ENTER with the highlight bar on each one. Then press the F12 key twice to begin your search.

Filtering takes longer, because the computer "filters" out only the records you have requested from the larger listing.

Exact Spelling. You may also want to narrow your search at times by using the EXACT SPELLING retrieval of surnames. For example, you may want to limit your search to look only at records with the exact spelling of the surname HARVIE from Nova Scotia. You would select the EXACT spelling filter option. You can select more than one filter for any search (but if it takes too long, it will not retrieve all possible names). Try it both ways. (See Figures 44A & B.)

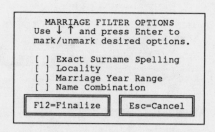

FIGURE 44B Filters Available with Marriage Search (International Genealogical Index)

2. *Holding File.* Records that you want to print or download can be placed in a holding file and copied as a group. (See Figure 45, (items E through I).

Sources

Millions of the records in the International Genealogical Index are part of the extraction program of the LDS Church, where Church members copy the pertinent genealogical information from selected records created by governments and churches for time periods when everyone is deceased, and enter them into a computer. The records are primarily births, christenings, and marriages. There are 94.5 million of them in the 1993 edition.

The *Parish and Vital Records List* (published on microfiche) shows which records have been extracted for each area and time period. But read the introduction to the new edition of this microfiche publication to see the changes in its relationship to the IGI.

The batch number prefix tells you the source for most entries. (Most alpha prefixes are from extraction, but there are exceptions such as "F" and "A"; and some numerical prefixes are also from extraction.) The source of the entry is identified in the compact disc edition of the index. You can see this by pressing ENTER while the detail window is displayed (see Figure 42). The introduction of the *IGI Batch Number Index* on microfiche lists all batch number prefixes and explains the meaning of each.

Millions of the names in the IGI come from records submitted by LDS Church members on their relatives, and from records of early LDS Church members who are now deceased.

The records are primarily for the time period of 1500-1900.

```
INDIVIDUAL SEARCH FILTERS
Use ↓ ↑ and press Enter to
mark/unmark desired options.

[ ] Exact Surname Spelling
[ ] Locality
[ ] Event Year Range

 F12=Finalize    Esc=Cancel
```

FIGURE 44A Filters Available with Individual Search

Geographical Coverage

The International Genealogical Index includes records from more than 90 countries. To see a list of regions, press the F11 function key; to see a list of countries/counties and which region they appear in, press the letter U while in the region index.

Editions and their Formats

The 1988 edition of the IGI was available on both microfiche and on compact disc. The 1992 edition contains 187 million names and is available only on microfiche. The 1993 edition has over 200 million names and is available only on compact disc.

Duplication

As you use the International Genealogical Index, you will notice that the same name frequently appears there more than once for the same person and for the same ordinances. Often, you can easily see that they are the same person, but the computer could not determine this. More advanced techniques now make it possible to match records that are nearly the same but different in some particulars. But this was not always true. If even one letter was different, then the computer was programmed to think it was a different person, and so the record was cleared again. And many times the record of an event is listed in more than one jurisdiction. For example, a person is born in Rockingham County, New Hampshire, but the family moves to Mt. Vernon, Kennebec, Maine, where the family is recorded there by the town clerk. There are vital records in both places that list the family. Computer checking to prevent duplication in temple work continues to limit searches to a state basis in the U. S. (county basis in England and many other countries), so there is no way such duplication can be avoided unless submitters personally look in the IGI, and then do not submit the names. (The compact disc edition brings together many of these duplicate records.) Another cause of increased duplication is that records that were processed in independent systems are now being added to the IGI.

Making Copies

Records can be printed from any of the screens (at least screen prints, which show just the screen you are looking at.) But records can be downloaded (copied) onto diskette only from the holding file.

To place records in the holding file, press the F2 key, then the letter E (create or add to holding file), and with the highlight bar on the record you want to include, press ENTER.

A small window will appear on your screen telling you the holding file is in operation. A small marker will appear temporarily next to the name on the screen, and the window will tell you how many records you have in the holding file. (You can place all names on the screen in the holding file by holding down the ALT key and pressing ENTER at the same time.) The holding file will usually hold up to 200 records (this is adjustable, according to the administrative decision of the library or center, and may be limited to a smaller number of records to allow more people use of the files). It cannot be changed by the user of the file.

You can delete an entry from the holding file by selecting F from the print/holding file menu, and placing the highlight bar on the name and pressing ENTER. The name will not disappear from your listing, but will be deleted from printing or downloading after you press the F12 key.

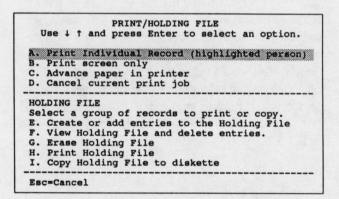

FIGURE 45 Print Menu also shows Holding File
(International Genealogical Index)

You can download with or without LDS ordinance dates; and with or without source references. If you want the information included, place an X beside the option.

To delete the records in the holding file, press F2, then G, then F12.

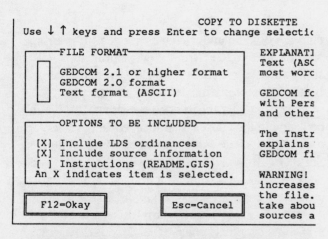

```
                  COPY TO DISKETTE
Use ↓ ↑ keys and press Enter to change selectio

    ┌FILE FORMAT─────────────┐    EXPLANATI
    │ ┌─┐                     │    Text (ASC
    │ │ │ GEDCOM 2.1 or higher format    most worc
    │ └─┘ GEDCOM 2.0 format   │
    │     Text format (ASCII) │    GEDCOM fc
    │                         │    with Pers
    └─────────────────────────┘    and other

    ┌OPTIONS TO BE INCLUDED──┐    The Instr
    │                         │    explains
    │ [X] Include LDS ordinances │  GEDCOM fi
    │ [X] Include source information │
    │ [ ] Instructions (README.GIS) │ WARNING!
    │ An X indicates item is selected. │ increases
    │                         │    the file.
    │ ┌─────────┐   ┌──────────┐ │   take abou
    │ │ F12=Okay│   │ Esc=Cancel│ │  sources a
    │ └─────────┘   └──────────┘ │
    └─────────────────────────┘
```

FIGURE 46 Tell the computer to include LDS ordinance detail by placing an X in the option box (International Genealogical Index)

Instructions will appear on the screen. Just follow them. And more help is available by pressing the F1 key while on that screen.

If you wish to make a paper printout of one record, press the A on the print/holding file menu (see Figure 45). When you have multiple records to print, after placing them in the holding file, press H, and then press F12 to finalize.

If you wish to download your records for use either on a word processor or in GEDCOM format for use with a personal computer using a genealogy software package that handles GEDCOM, select the option identified as the letter I. You will need to have a formatted diskette. It may be possible to purchase one from the family history center, or you may need to bring one with you to the center.

In Summary

1. Be wise in how and what you download

2. Understand the file, and what you get and how

    • Use the Parent Index, the Individual Index, and the Marriage Index to best accomplish your task.

    • Look for the name of a person in the Individual Index and see how the parents' names are listed.

    • Press the F8 key to choose the Parent Index, and then the F12 key to accept the parents' names exactly as shown in the Individual Index and see how many of the children's records this brings together.

    • If they are not all brought together, look for names using the parent's name in different ways: (Thomas Stones and Sarah Newton.); list the

mother's name first (Sarah Newton and Thomas Stones); without using the mother's maiden surname (Thomas Stones and Sarah); without using any name for the mother; (Thomas Stones); using variations of the father's name. (T. John Stones, T. J. Stones, or John Stones.)

• Use the filter option to limit the records retrieved to those of one state or one county (for some countries), when appropriate.

Downloading from the Parent Index often will allow you to quickly retrieve and copy the records of obvious brothers and sisters. (Watch also for records of other persons who are not related, but whose parents have the same names.)

But downloading from the Parent Index will **not** retrieve marriage records nor children with no parent listed. You must go into the other indexes and retrieve these records.

Review the common characteristics of the resource files on page 2 to understand what names will be brought together. (And watch for updates in the programs that may change some things.)

Special Helps for Members of The Church of Jesus Christ of Latter-day Saints (LDS)

The purpose for which the International Genealogical Index is created is to help members of The Church of Jesus Christ of Latter-day Saints avoid duplication in research and temple ordinances for their ancestors.

1. *Locating Ordinances.* It requires locating two entries to obtain the four LDS ordinances for a person. The baptism, endowment, and sealing to parents dates are listed as part of the birth or christening record; the sealing of husband and wife is listed as part of the marriage record. There is no link in the file between these two records for the same person(s).

2. *Surnames for Women.* Women are almost always listed under their maiden surnames. However, there are a small percentage of cases where the maiden surname was not known, or a previous married surname was thought to be the maiden surname, and the temple ordinances were performed under the married surname. Sometimes these are indicated with a MRS. attached, but often they are not. If you don't find the person you are looking for under her

maiden surname, you may find her under a married surname. When a widow remarries, she is of course married under her previous husband's surname, which is her legal surname at that time. But if her maiden surname is known, it may appear in the International Genealogical Index under her maiden surname. Also look under given names with no surname, by typing only the given name and pressing F12.

3. *Examples of entries* that list the married surname of the woman for her baptism and endowment:

- Many town records in Maine, New Hampshire, and Massachusetts in particular list the entire family. The wife and mother is listed only by her married surname. Beginning with the 1988 edition of the IGI, the accompanying name is identified as her spouse, and this gives you a clue that this is her married surname.
  Example: Abigail Wilbur, born 1757 in Massachusetts, is the wife of Joseph Wilbur. Her maiden surname is not known.
- Cemetery records are sometimes used for "vital records," especially when they have been included in printed vital records. But these records list women by their married surnames. Example: Mary Fyans in Massachusetts is the wife of Thomas Fyans. Her maiden name of Craig is not listed. A study of the publication from which the entry was taken will tell you that it was a cemetery record that was used for the "vital record" information.
- Descendants have not known for sure (or at all) what the maiden surname is, and have submitted the name under the married surname.
- Early LDS branch and ward records may not have included the maiden surname. Example, Encora Woodcock is listed as Encora Batty.

4. *Variations Across Files*. It is also possible that her name may be different in Ancestral File than it is in the International Genealogical Index. This is especially true in the marriage records. For example, Amanda was the daughter of Wesley Jones. She married first Milton White, second Robert Smith, and third Thomas Brown. The marriage records for the different marriages would identify her as Amanda Jones, marrying Milton White; Amanda White marrying Robert Smith; and Amanda Smith marrying Thomas Brown. (Her birth

record would be under Amanda Jones.) If marriage records are extracted from vital records, they will show only the previous husband's surname for her. If they are submitted by descendants they will probably list only the maiden surname. She would be found in the census records according to her legal name at that time--which could be Jones, White, Smith, or Brown. She will possibly be buried under her last husband's name, but may be buried beside any one of her husbands, and identified with his surname. Look under all possibilities, and don't reject an entry just because the name is different from what you expected. (But don't force matches where they don't exist.)

5. *Special Reports of Missing Ordinances on Ancestors*. It is possible to print a report listing ancestors and their children who are missing any LDS ordinance date. Such a report can be printed from Ancestral File or from Personal Ancestral File. (This does not mean the ordinance has not been done.)

6. *Clues*

- Prior to 1969 when the "single entry" method of name submission was adopted by the Church, no marriage sealing could be done until the baptism and endowment had already been done. Therefore, if you have a sealing to spouse date for an individual before 1970, you know that the baptism and endowment have been done for that person, and do not need to be done again. This can be important in avoiding duplication of ordinances, because about three million of those early marriage sealings (those where the sealing record included the date and place of legal marriage) were extracted from the early temple records and added to the International Genealogical Index in the 1970s. But the baptism and endowment records for those individuals may not yet have been added. By understanding the processing policies and guidelines that were in effect at that time, you can know that it is done, and not repeat it. (The baptisms and endowments are in process of being automated and added to the IGI.

Caution. Some marriage entries may be misleading. For most temples in the earlier time period, if the date and place of original marriage were not included in the temple record it was not extracted (automated) from the original temple record in the 1970s. However, especially for the Endowment House in early Salt Lake City, many were extracted listing the date and place of *sealing* for the date and place of marriage. Thus, the couple may appear to be married many years after many of their children were born, and in a different place. (These types of entries usually have M17 or M18 as the beginning of the batch number.)

• When a probate record or a U.S or Canadian census record was used for submitting names for temple ordinances during the years 1969-1978, no ordinances were done for the parents. And even though the name of the father's wife was listed in the original record, it was not included in the automated record. (This was because it was not known whether she was the mother of his children, because the wives so often died and the husbands remarried.) This means that the name of a wife, (possibly the mother) may be found by going to the original record.

• From 1969-1978, census records for the United States and Canada were acceptable sources for the following: *1850, 1851,* all persons listed in the family (except children born in New England where birth records were assumed to exist), except the parents (adults listed with the children were included); *1860, 1861,* those children 10 years old and under (because those over 10 were assumed to be listed in the *1850, 1851,* census). The place of the event listed in the IGI for these census entries is the *place of residence* when the census was taken, and *not* the place of birth.

• Studies were done in many areas to determine surnames not brought together in the standard spellings, but which contained records for the same families. These appear in the microfiche version of the IGI as "see also" references.

• The IGI does not include many marriage records for the New England states of Connecticut, New Hampshire, or Vermont. (Check the *Parish and Vital Records List* to see what records are included in the extraction program.) .

• Many Ancestral File records will not include the date of sealing to parents or the sealing to spouse. This doesn't necessarily mean it has not been done, nor that the person who submitted it did not have the date. It may instead reflect the amount of information that could be placed on the submission forms used for the base of Ancestral File. These were the old-style, legal sized family group records and pedigree charts. There was space on the family group record for only three ordinances--either baptism, endowment, and sealing to parents (when the person was listed as a child on the form), or baptism, endowment, and sealing to spouse (when the person was listed as a parent (husband or wife) on the form. Thus, the forms did not have a space to record the sealing-to-parents date for the last generation submitted by a descendant, or the sealing-to-spouse date for those listed only as a child on a family group record. And since the International Genealogical Index does not yet include the early sealing to parents dates, and many of the early sealing of couples, you should contact those submitters before you submit the names for sealings. Otherwise, unnecessary duplication will result. (It is, of course, a personal decision of what you want to do. But the chances are great that these sacred ordinances have already been done.)

• For early LDS pioneer families, look at the sealing date of the parents. If the parents were sealed as a couple before the child was born (and the parents were NOT excommunicated before the birth), that child has a birthright blessing of being born in the covenant (BIC), and does not need to be sealed to parents. The BIC status may need to be added to the Ancestral File or International Genealogical Index record.

• Early dates for sealing of children to parents also indicate clues that may lead to additional records. The temple sealing records of children to parents will often show the entire family. And there is often a family group record in the two "old" patrons sections family group records--those submitted in the 1920s and in the 1960s. Whether you would benefit from using these sources depends on your need.

• Most of the Temple records of proxy baptisms performed prior to 1942 have been added to the International Genealogical Index. These records can be very valuable because they often listed entire family groups and sometimes all of the known relatives of the early LDS converts. While it took more time to do an endowment, the baptisms were often done at the same time, and can provide valuable facts and clues for the family historian. (names of people and places may have been spelled phonetically).

- Many baptism and endowment ordinances have been done for persons who lived in the 1500 and 1600s, based on their marriage records. These appear in the International Genealogical Index under their marriage date, with an event code of S (miscellaneous). There is no need for these ordinances to be performed again, but you must be alert to recognize them as your ancestors. (Future editions of the index may give them estimated birth dates. Watch for changes in the way records may be displayed.)

- The names of many of those who joined the LDS Church in the early days were extracted from the early LDS branch and ward records, and sent to the temple to have ordinances performed for them. The identifiers in these records are often different from what you would expect. Sometimes the baptism date was used in lieu of a birth date (and occasionally the baptism was performed again, by mistake); the place where they were living at that time may have been used for the event place. A woman may have been listed in the records by her married surname, and may appear in the index under her married surname. However, if the record refers to her father's name, this was assumed to be her maiden surname and she will be listed in this index under this name, even though she is not listed in the early ward and branch records by that name. Occasionally the term MRS is added to the record where the surname is known to be her husband's surname, but not always.

7. *From 1969-1978*, it was not possible to submit a name for temple ordinances that did not have at least a year of birth, christening or marriage and two levels of place descriptions (such as county and state or country). (The exception was the probate records and U.S. and Canadian census records, which were submitted as "document dates".)

Beginning in 1978, it was again possible to submit names without having the complete information. At this time, the use of document dates to identify persons was discontinued, and estimated ("about") dates and "of" places (where a person lived) were used. These names were processed through a different system, and were not checked against the

International Genealogical Index. These records have batch numbers that begin with the letter F. There are only 4.5 million of these records.

In these records a person was identfied based on either the spouse and children or the parents and siblings (brothers and sisters). Thus, they could have very different identifiers for the same person. For temple ordinances, the names of relatives were used as part of the identifiers in duplicate checking within that system, though estimated dates and places of residence were also used. (If the names of both spouse and parents were submitted at the same time, the ordinances of baptism and endowment and sealing to parents were done with the identifiers based on the parents and siblings; the marriage record was based on the spouse and children, though in this case the estimated dates and places would be the same in both records.) If not enough children or siblings were listed, other identifiers were added as children-perhaps names of grandparents or aunts or uncles, or in-laws; occasionally a name of a relative was made up to make a "unique identification." (You will find these extra names on the submission documents if you trace the batch number--though it is not always easy to tell when they were not included by the submitter; but these names are not in the IGI.) Don't miss your entries because they appear a little different from what you may expect.

Although the names were submitted on family group forms, the relationship of family members was not retained in the file. That is, there is no link between the record of a child and the records for his parents. *However, the batch and sheet number may be the same. (Names on the form that had complete information will have a slightly different batch number.)*

Note: Many of these may be in families, with ordinance dates, in Ancestral File, because the families have submitted them there.

8. *Explanation.* While it is true that these temple ordinances need to be done only once for each person, there is no harm done when an ordinance is repeated for that person. (It only means that another is still waiting to receive their ordinances.) We are encouraged to do careful ordinance checking where feasible, to avoid unnecessary duplication. The person who gives unselfish service will be blessed for that effort, regardless of whether the ordinance is needed or has already been done. As the

responsibility for ordinance checking is transferred from Church headquarters to the members, it becomes an individual responsibility for each submitter to determine whether or not the ordinances have already been performed for a given deceased person. TempleReady will help, but members still need to be involved. The computer will never stop a lot of the duplication that a person can know and avoid.

9. *Role of Ancestral File.* The place to bring all of this together is in Ancestral File, where an individual is identified by his own dates and places of events, and associated with all his family members.

Ordinance dates in Ancestral File. These were submitted by members of the Church on their ancestors and other relatives. In my opinion, if an ordinance date is listed in Ancestral File, the chances that ordinances have been done are very near 100%. The date may be off a few days (or in some cases, even a few years). But is that important? All we need to know is that the ordinance has been done, and does not need to be done again.

The question may also arise as to how important it is to determine the earliest date for baptism, endowment, or sealing. If our purpose is to ensure that the ordinances have been done, it does not matter when they were done. However, for persons who were members of the Church in life, it may have meaning. For example, if a couple were sealed before the birth of a child, that child does not need to be sealed to his parents. Also, the earlier ordinance dates may be helpful from a research point of view, because the information may have been provided by the persons during their lifetimes, or by someone with personal knowledge of the events and relationships. If you have two dates for an ordinance, it is usually best to use the earlier one.

For the Non-LDS, an Explanation

Members of The Church of Jesus Christ of Latter-day Saints believe in life after death and that family relationships are meant to be eternal. They believe that ordinances performed in temples are necessary to eternal progression, but these must be performed in this world by someone who has authority from Jesus Christ. Therefore, for persons who did not have the opportunity in this life to receive these ordinances of baptism,

endowment and "sealing" into family relationships, someone else can act for that person and receive these blessing by proxy in their behalf. The deceased person is then free to accept or reject the ordinance. Each Church member has a responsibility to receive these blessings for himself or herself during his/her lifetime, and then to see that his/her ancestors have had their ordinances performed. The Church has the responsibility to assist the members in doing this, and to keep a record of the ordinances that are performed.

For more information on the 1993 edition of the International Genealogical Index, see page 56 and the inside and outside back covers of this publication.

SOCIAL SECURITY DEATH INDEX

The Social Security Death Index is a file of over 47 million brief records made available by the United States government through the Freedom of Information Act. The government began to automate their Social Security death notices in 1962. Therefore, the file covers mostly records where deaths were reported during the period 1962-1993.

Record Elements

1. *Names.* Only the first given name or initial and a surname is recorded. This brief information is taken from the way name was listed on the Social Security record at the time of death. This means a woman will almost always be found under her married surname at that time.

2. *Dates.* The full birth and death dates are usually listed.

3. *Places.* The place where the person was living when he or she applied for a Social Security number is listed.

4. *The last legal place of residence is listed.* (Note: This is not necessarily the place of death.)

5. *The place where the death benefit was mailed*, as determined by the zip code, may also be included.

6. *No names of relatives* are included in the file.

```
              Social Security Death Index 1.07         06 FEB 1991
    Esc=Exit  F1=Help  F2=Print/Holding File  F4=Search  F5=Record Offices
╔════════════════════════════════════════════════════════════════════════╗
║ PgDn PgUp and press Enter for details.                                   ║
║                                                                          ║
║    Name (-Name Group-)          Birth  Issuance Place  Death  Residence  ║
║ ┌─────────────────────────────────────────────────────────────────────┐║
║ │-NICHOLS-                                                              │║
║ │    Clyde NICHOLS ............. 1901  Kentucky        1984  Kentucky   │║
║ │    Clyde NICHOLS ............. 1901  New Hampshire   1963  New Hampshire│║
║ │    Clyde NICHOLS ............. 1901  Oklahoma        1983  Oklahoma   │║
║ │    Clyde NICHOLS ............. 1902  Oklahoma        1980  Texas      │║
║ │    Clyde NICHOLS ............. 1902  South Carolina  1979  North Carolina│║
║ │    Clyde NICHOLS ............. 1902  Texas           1972  Texas      │║
║ │    Clyde NICHOLLS ............ 1902  Washington      1980  Oregon     │║
║ │    Clyde NICHOLS ............. 1903  California      1965             │║
║ │    Clyde NICHOLAS ............ 1903  Colorado        1981  Colorado   │║
║ │    Clyde NICHOLS ............. 1903  Missouri        1988  Washington │║
║ │    Clyde NICKLAS ............. 1903  Pennsylvania    1979  Pennsylvania│║
║ │    Clyde NICHOLS ............. 1904  Arkansas        1981  Arkansas   │║
║ │    Clyde NICKEL .............. 1904  Iowa            1966             │║
║ │    Clyde NICHOLLS ............ 1904  Michigan        1985  Florida    │║
║ │    Clyde NICHOLS ............. 1904  Ohio            1979  Ohio       │║
║ │    Clyde NICHOLAS ............ 1904  West Virginia   1968  West Virginia│║
║ └─────────────────────────────────────────────────────────────────────┘║
╚════════════════════════════════════════════════════════════════════════╝
```

FIGURE 47 Index List (Social Security Death Index)

Display

The general display is the same as in the other genealogical resource files. There is an alphabetical index, which lists brief information. By pressing ENTER, a detail window opens that shows all genealogical information (see Figure 48). By pressing ENTER a second time, the zip code information is displayed (see Figure 49).

The same options of filtering, using exact or similar surnames in retrieval, and the holding file are available.

Making Copies

You can make paper copies of the information or download to diskette by following the instructions listed.

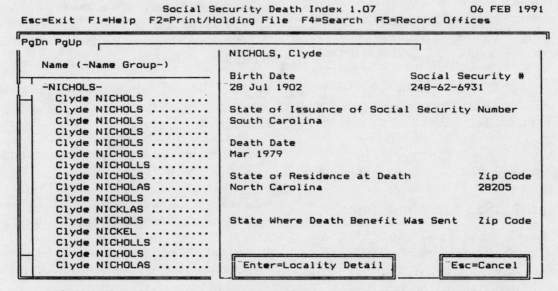

FIGURE 48 Index screen with detail window open (Social Security Death Index)

```
                 Social Security Death Index 1.07          06 FEB 1991
       Esc=Exit  F1=Help  F2=Print/Holding File  F4=Search  F5=Record Offices
     ╔═══════════════════════════════════════════════════════════════════════════╗
      PgDn PgUp   ┌─────────────────────────────────────────────────┐
     ║           │ NICHOLS, Clyde                                    │             ║
      ┌──────────┴─────────────────────────────────────────────────┴───────────┐
      │                    LOCALITY DETAIL                                       │
      │                                                                          │
      │      Press F5 to see where to send for birth and death certificates.     │
      │      Press TAB to move between columns.  Use  to scroll.                 │
      │                                                                   │      │
      │      Death Residence Localities          Death Benefit Localities        │
      ├──────────────────────────────────────────┬─────────────────────────────┤
      │  28205                                    │                             │
      │  Charlotte, Mecklenburg, North Caroli     │                             │
      │                                           │                             │
      │                                           │                             │
      │                                           │                             │
      │                                           │                             │
      │                                           │                             │
      ├───────────────────────────────────────────┴────────────┬────────────────┤
      │  The locality information is based on zip codes.         │ ┌────────────┐│
      │  The zip codes may include more than one locality.       │ │ Esc=Cancel ││
      │                                                          │ └────────────┘│
      └──────────────────────────────────────────────────────────┴────────────────┘
```

FIGURE 49 Index screen with locality detail window open (Social Security Death Index)

1. Locality information in paper copies. In making paper copies from the holding file, the locality (place) information is limited. You get full locality information by making an individual print, or in the download, but not from the holding file.

   In uploading the records into the Personal Ancestral File (or other software program), you will not have linked records. You will need to link them together, where appropriate.

2. Additional Helps:

   • Not all people had Social Security numbers in the earlier days of the program's existence. In addition, some were involved in separate retirement programs, such as railroad workers and government employees, and were not eligible for Social Security. Therefore, their deaths would not be reported (even though some may have had a Social Security number).

   • For those whose records are found, additional information may be available from the Social Security records. There is a charge for such a search: When the social security number is known, there is a $7 search fee for a copy of the form filled in when the person applied for the Social Security number. (When using that information, be careful. The person often gave the information to a clerk, who wrote it down. Errors do exist. For example, a person who was self-employed is listed as unemployed. Similar mistakes in dates and places may occur.)

   If the person has died within the last five years, there may also be information supplied at the time of death. There is an additional charge of $14 for this search, plus photocopy expense if anything is found. These records are usually kept only for five years and then destroyed.

   Send requests to: Freedom of Information Officer, 4-H-8 Annex Building, 6401 Security Blvd, Baltimore, MD 21235.

3. There is usually a death certificate available created by the state and often also by the town where the person died. Death certificates usually include the names of parents and the date and place of birth, which is helpful but not always correct. The address of where to write for death certificates for each state is provided as part of FamilySearch. To have this displayed, press the F5 key, move the highlight bar to the name of the state, and press ENTER.

   • There is also usually an obituary in the place where the person last resided. You may want to use the zip code listed in the Index, and select a library in that area. Then visit or write to them. If you write, ask them to search their local papers for an obituary about that date. Enclose a check for a small amount, perhaps $5. Most libraries are very helpful with this type of request. Obituaries usually give information on birth, death, parents, sometimes brief historical facts, and names and residences of survivors. It may also list the place of burial (which can lead to sexton and cemetery records), and often the name of the mortuary, which can lead to additional records.

- Remember that the zip code was used to determine place of residence at time of death. Sometimes the zip code may refer to several different places. For example, 84037 is listed as the zip code on my mother's place of residence at death. The places given refer to Kaysville, Utah (where one of her sons was living at that time and where her mail was being sent), and Fruit Heights, Utah. But she actually died in a hospital in Bountiful, Utah, after a long illness there. (All of these places are in Davis County.) The state is correct, and the zip code can help narrow the specific town where more records may be available. (In this case, all places are near Salt Lake City, where the obituary is found.) The obituary indicates that burial was in Charlotte, North Carolina--a valuable clue if this information was not already known. It also states that she was born in Iowa--giving another valuable clue, because her Social Security number was issued in North Carolina. The obituary also states that she was a member of The Church of Jesus Christ of Latter-day Saints--offering another option for obtaining additional information.

- As in all records, allow for a margin of error. Use the valuable information provided, but don't miss entries with clues because the information is not exactly as you expect, and don't limit your searches too strictly to exactly the information provided. (Become a detective, and enjoy the process.)

USING DOWNLOADED RECORDS

Uploading Records into Personal Ancestral File

The Personal Ancestral File (PAF) is a genealogy software package for use on home computers. It is available for MS DOS (IBM and compatible) in version 2.3 and MacIntosh in version 2.1. It has previously been available for Apple II in version 2.0, but the Apple II version is no longer available. Only the MS DOS version 2.3 is completely updated and capable of doing all that we will be discussing. It is an inexpensive program ($35), but has many capabilities. (See glossary.)

The steps for uploading records into the Personal Ancestral File are basically the same for Ancestral File, International Genealogical Index, and Social Security Death Index (and any other file that produces GEDCOM formatted records). However, once they are uploaded, there are some differences.

First, you must determine what you want to do. It is recommended that you create a temporary working file to place your records in, and not put them in the same file or directory as your family records are stored. Each data file has its own directory where the computer stores the data either on hard disk or on a floppy diskette.

You almost always need to examine your GEDCOM records and then decide what you want to add to your own family records file. Therefore, you want to create a temporary directory or file to hold the records while you study them.

```
------------------------
PERSONAL ANCESTRAL FILE
------------------------
Release 2.3 (22 Nov 1993)

        ACCESS MENU

1. Family Records
2. Genealogical Information Exchange
3. Research Data Filer
4. Family Records Check
5. Family Records Check/Repair
6. Configure Programs
0. Return to System

Please enter your selection:
```

FIGURE 50 Access Menu (Personal Ancestral File, 2.3)

When you upload your records into PAF in the Genealogical Information Exchange portion of PAF (see option 2 in Figure 50), you can either add it to an existing data file by typing in the name of that file, or create a new file by typing in a name that has never yet been used for a file name on your disk (such as TEMP) see figure 57. The computer will create a new file for you.

If you have forgotten what you named the GEDCOM file, press F3 and select from the GEDCOM files displayed by Pressing F1. (The GEDCOM files displayed will be those on the drive you specified (see line two of figure 57). Be sure these match the drive your GEDCOM files are on, usually A, B, or C.

When you have more than one GEDCOM file, each one must be added to your TEMP file, following the procedures outlined. You may want to make a screen print of the file names, so you can check them off as they are uploaded. (A copy of the records is uploaded into your PAF, but the GEDCOM file remains on your disk until you delete it or format over it.)

If you have selected the option to have the listing file information placed in the notes of each record (an option in the permanent configuration), any names of persons or places that are too long for PAF fields, or dates that included things like "age 80" will be easily accessible to the record to which they refer.

```
                    TEMPORARY CONFIGURATION
                    -----------------------
        Computer selected: IBM PC, XT, AT, PS/2 or fully compatible
         Printer selected: Epson EX/LQ & New FX
      Drive for Data Disk: c:\paf\temp\
   Drive for Program Disk: c:\paf\
   Drive for Scratch Disk: c:

                    Require a carriage return on menus? (Y/N): N
    Force surnames to uppercase on Family Records reports? (Y/N): Y
                    Use form feeds when printing? (Y/N): N
                              Parallel printer port: 1
        Enter the full path and name of your communications package (optional):
           [                                                    ]
   Screen Color (optional):              Normal  Bold  Reverse  Help
                        Characters (00-15):   7     15     0      0
                        Background (00-07):   0      0     7      2
   Color codes:
      00 Black  03 Cyan     06 Brown  09 L. Blue   12 L. Red     15. Bright
      01 Blue   04 Red      07 White  10 L. Green  13 L. Magenta     White
      02 Green  05 Magenta  08 Grey   11 L. Cyan   14 Yellow

   F1 SAVE CHANGES AND CONTINUE     F2 QUIT
```

FIGURE 51 Item 3 shows the "path" for the directory or file where the computer is going to store this data (Personal Ancestral File, 2.2)

```
                    TEMPORARY CONFIGURATION
                    -----------------------
        Computer selected: IBM PC, XT, AT, PS/2 or fully compatible
         Printer selected: Epson EX/LQ & New FX
      Drive for Data Disk: b:
   Drive for Program Disk: a:
   Drive for Scratch Disk: a:

                    Require a carriage return on menus? (Y/N): N
    Force surnames to uppercase on Family Records reports? (Y/N): Y
                    Use form feeds when printing? (Y/N): N
                              Parallel printer port: 1
        Enter the full path and name of your communications package (optional):
           [                                                    ]
   Screen Color (optional):              Normal  Bold  Reverse  Help
                        Characters (00-15):   7     15     0      0
                        Background (00-07):   0      0     7      2
   Color codes:
      00 Black  03 Cyan     06 Brown  09 L. Blue   12 L. Red     15. Bright
      01 Blue   04 Red      07 White  10 L. Green  13 L. Magenta     White
      02 Green  05 Magenta  08 Grey   11 L. Cyan   14 Yellow

   F1 SAVE CHANGES AND CONTINUE     F2 QUIT
```

FIGURE 52 When the computer has two floppy disk drives (rather than a hard disk), you tell the computer, by what you type on this screen, which drive contains each floppy diskettes. (Personal Ancestral File, 2.2)

```
                    -----------------------
                    PERSONAL ANCESTRAL FILE
                    -----------------------

                         UTILITIES MENU

      1. Add/Change Patron Name and Address
      2. Add/Change Printed Reports Title
      3. Temporarily Change Configuration
      4. Statistics
      5. Back up Data Files To Diskette
      6. Restore Data Files From Backup Disk
      7. Check Data Files
      8. Fix Data Files
      0. Return to Main Menu

         Please enter your selection:
```

FIGURE 53 Family Records Utilities Menu (Personal Ancestral File, 2.3)

In version 2.2 you had to go into Family Records to create a new data base; in version 2.3 you do not. You can create a new one in the Genealogical Information Exchange section. This change has made a difference in the flow of these steps.

To upload your records into PAF, follow these steps:

1. Choose the Genealogical Information Exchange (GIE) section, which is option 2 on the Main Access Menu. (See Figure 50.)

2. Next select option 3, "Genealogical Data Communications (GEDCOM) (see Figure 54.)

```
------------------------------------
      GENEALOGICAL INFORMATION EXCHANGE
------------------------------------

                MAIN MENU

1. Ancestral File Submission
2. Temple Names Submission
3. Genealogical Data Communications (GEDCOM)
0. Return to System

        Please enter your selection:
```

FIGURE 54 Main Menu in Genealogical Information Exchange (Personal Ancestral File, 2.2)

3. From the next menu, choose option 2, *Add All GEDCOM Files. . .*

```
------------------------------------
      GENEALOGICAL DATA COMMUNICATIONS
------------------------------------

              GEDCOM MENU

1. Create GEDCOM File
2. Add All of GEDCOM File to Family Records Data
3. Add Part of GEDCOM File to Family Records Data
4. Send/Receive GEDCOM File
5. Print GEDCOM File
0. Return to Main Menu

        Please enter your selection:
```

FIGURE 55 GEDCOM Menu (Personal Ancestral File)

A warning screen will appear, telling you the records may be scrambled. You have no records in this directory or file, so press F1 and continue. But watch the screen as you continue, to be sure it shows the name of the directory you want to be working in. (If you do have records in the directory, you should have a backup copy of the data, in case your records are damaged. They rarely are, but it is better to have no regrets. You can easily make a backup copy by inserting a formatted diskette and pressing the F2 key, if you have a hard disk.)

When the name of the default file is shown (for example, C:\PAF\NICHOLS [see line 1 of Figure 51], type over the name of your default data file where your family records are stored, in this case NICHOLS, with TEMP (or whatever name you are giving your temporary working file), then delete the extra letters. IMPORTANT: Be sure the screen now displays the file name you want the records added to.

Your GEDCOM file usually will be in drive A:, so you need to type the letter A followed by a colon (**A:**) on line 2.

```
------------------------------------
      ADD GEDCOM TO FAMILY RECORDS DATA
------------------------------------

                WARNING!

Your Family Records data can become scrambled
if GIE aborts before completing all its work!
Before you continue, create a BACKUP of your
Family Records data!




F1 CONTINUE        F2 QUIT     F3 MAKE BACKUP OF DATA
```

FIGURE 56 Warning screen allow you to decide to make a backup copy, when needed (Personal Ancestral File, 2.3)

```
------------------------------------
      ADD GEDCOM TO FAMILY RECORDS DATA
------------------------------------

  Family Records Data Disk: C:\PAF\TEMP\
        (Target Path)

      GEDCOM File Disk: A:
        (Source Path)

    Name of GEDCOM File: HARVIE

Name of GEDCOM Listing File:
        The listing file will contain a report of any
        problems that may occur when you add a GEDCOM file
        to your Family Records data.  The listing file has
        the name you enter plus a .LST extension.

Reuse deleted records? (Y/N) N


F1 CONTINUE        F2 QUIT     F3 SELECT GEDCOM FILE
```

FIGURE 57 Preparing to add GEDCOM file to a data file named TEMP (data file on a hard disk; GEDCOM file on a diskette in drive A—Personal Ancestral File, 2.3)

On line 3, type whatever name you gave the GEDCOM file when you created it (perhaps you used HARVIE), then press the F1 key, and your records will be added. (The computer will add the name of the listing file, which is the same as the GEDCOM file.)

Listing File

Field lengths in PAF are fixed. That means that only 16 characters (letters or symbols such as (?,) can be in a field for names of persons and places, and dates that include words like "16 Jun 1882, age 93" will not fit in PAF. But Ancestral File and other files may have variable length fields that will contain more than 16 letters in a name, or added information in a date. PAF cuts off the words. For example, an IGI place that

44

states **Saint John Episcopal Church, Elizabeth, Union, New Jersey** will list only **Saint John Episc** in the first field of the place. In PAF, the listing file will record the entire information. PAF will put it either into a listing file, or into the notes for each person. It depends on how you configure your PAF program when you load it. (You probably want it in the notes.)

To have the listing file automatically put into the notes field for each record. Saves many hours of time for a large file, especially if there is duplication and some records are merged.. To do this, mark Y for yes on the permanent CONFIGURATION screen to the question: "When importing records, put listing file messages in notes?" This author highly recommends saying YES to this question. You will then have the information on what the whole name of a place or person or entire date field (including "age 80") accessible to each record right in the notes.

How to Get Selected Records Merged, Edited and Ready to Add into Your Main Data File

To study the records you have just uploaded into the TEMP file:

1. Go back into the Family Records section, and go into your new working file. (To do this, from the main Family Records Menu, select A (Utilities) and 3 (Temporarily change. . .) See Figure 53. Type over what is there with the name of your temporary file, such as TEMP and delete the others letters (change C:\PAF\NICHOLS\ to read C:\PAF\TEMP\). Now press F1 twice; press zero once, and it will take you to the main Family Records Menu (see Figure 60). Press 4 (pedigree search) and you will be viewing your data.

2. Review your records and get a feel for what is there.

3. You can now do searches on any element that is in the file. Or you can look at an alphabetical listing of all the names in the file by pressing a 1 while in the Pedigree Search option. Or press an H and fill in the blanks. For example, locate the entry for James Harvie, born 1746 (see Figure 6.) But if he is listed in your data as James HARVEY, this would require an additional search. And a search for **James Harvie** would not retrieve the **Jas** Harvie entry. The Personal Ancestral File will retrieve only on exact details.

```
                          INDIVIDUAL DATA                    (Search)
          ------------------------------------------------------------------
          Sex:      SURNAME:           Given1:                      RIN:
                    Given2:            Given3:          Title:
          ------------------------------------------------------------------
          BIRTH        Date:
            PLACE  Level 1:                     Level 2:
                   Level 3:                     Level 4:
          CHRISTENING Date:
            PLACE      L 1:                      L 2:
                       L 3:                      L 4:
          DEATH        Date:
            PLACE      L 1:                      L 2:
                       L 3:                      L 4:
          BURIAL       Date:
            PLACE      L 1:                      L 2:
                       L 3:                      L 4:
          ------------------------------------------------------------------
          BAPTISM    Date:            Temple Code:
          ENDOWMENT  Date:            Temple Code:
          SEAL to PAR Date:           Temple Code:     ID NO.:
          ------------------------------------------------------------------
          Please input fields you want to search on.
          F1 BEGIN SEARCH      F2 QUIT WITHOUT SEARCHING
```

Figure 58 Data entry/search screen (Personal Ancestral File, 2.2)

The Personal Ancestral File can be configured (permanently or temporarily) to display or not display the bottom part of the screen, which provides for LDS ordinances of baptism, endowment, and sealing to parents, and for the marriage detail screen to provide space for sealing of couples. Answer the question yes or no in either the permanent config (configuration) program or in the temporarily change configuration feature as shown. (See Figure 59.)

```
                    TEMPORARY CONFIGURATION
                    -----------------------
              Verify new names during data entry? (Y/N): Y
         Ask "create notes?" after saving individual? (Y/N): Y
  Use separate files for notes rather than usual notes file? (Y/N): N
       Name of your notes editing program: [
         Match names AND positions during individual search? (Y/N): N
            Sort names for alphabetic browse before display? (Y/N): Y
             Starting RIN in Pedigree Search (0 for last used RIN): 1
          Show LDS ordinance fields on screens and reports? (Y/N): Y   ◀────

                Print numbers (R=RIN & MRIN, I=ID No., N=None): R
                    Print all notes on Family Group Records? (Y/N): N
      How many generations on letter-size pedigree charts? (4/5/6): 4
                    Paper type (C=continuous, S=single, ?=ask): C
                      Paper size (L=letter, G=legal, ?=ask): L

       LEFT-SIDE PRINTING MARGIN          PRINT CHARACTER FOR
           Normal-size print:               double line: 61
            Elite-size print:               single line: 45
       Compressed-size print:             vertical line: 124


  F1 SAVE CHANGES AND EXIT     F2 QUIT WITHOUT SAVING CHANGES
```

FIGURE 59 To display LDS ordinance dates on screens and/or reports, have line 8 show Y; to not even show the space for them, have it show N (Personal Ancestral File)

Frequencies of names of persons and places is an interesting listing that you can view by going to Facts and Fun from the main Family Records Menu.

Or you can go into FOCUS (option no. 7 on the main Family Records menu, see Figure 60) , and create your own requests--based on any element in either the record or the notes. This will allow you the possibility of bringing together records on a parish or county or farm name or batch number basis, as well as names or dates. (To bring them together on a batch number basis, use the "Add by matching data" and then "Add by matching notes"

4. You can remove much duplication from your file by using the matching function, and merging records. (This function is available only in MS DOS version.) You can do some of this by using the automatic match function. You can also print a list of possible matches and study them, then use the "manual" match (which also has a feature to automatically look for possible matches). While the automatic match will sometimes work, it sometimes fails to bring matches together. Usually you will need to use both approaches to complete what you want to accomplish.

You always have a choice, even in the automatic match. You must tell the computer whether to merge the records. You can also choose whether to merge the notes.

PAF 2.3 has an additional option "Merge individuals with matching IDs". See summary on inside back cover.

```
  ---------------------------
      PERSONAL ANCESTRAL FILE
  ---------------------------

            MAIN MENU

   1. Add Records
   2. Modify Records
   3. Delete Records
   4. Pedigree Search
   5. Notes
   6. Print Forms and Reports
   7. Focus/Design Reports
   8. Match/Merge
   9. Facts and Fun
   A. Utilities
   0. Return to System
  Please enter your selection:
```

FIGURE 60 Family Records Main Menu, Choose option 8 to match and merge your records (Personal Ancestral File)

Merges are made by pressing two keys at the same time: the shift key and the number 1 (which is the exclamation point [!]).

Records uploaded from Ancestral File are already pedigree-linked. However, there may be multiple copies of the same record in your download. This usually happens for one of two reasons: you downloaded in sections, and have an overlap in the records obtained; or your ancestry goes back to the same person more than once, as in the case of cousins marrying cousins. The file will download the same ancestor's record each time. This is especially troublesome when royalty lines are downloaded. It is not uncommon to go back to the same kings five or six or more times, once you tie into those lineages. You will want to remove this duplication before you add the records to your own family records file.

When you add them to your own family records, you may still have two records for one ancestor that need to be merged. For example, if you download the records from Ancestral File, and add them to the data base, perhaps you already had the record of James Harvie, born 1746. He is a direct ancestor, along with his daughter Margaret. But you did not have all of his children or all of his ancestors' records. You need to merge the incoming record for him with the one already in the file.

To do this, select option 8 from the main Family Records menu (see Figure 60). As you merge the two records for him, it will link his ancestors and descendants in the file. (If you use the delete function to remove one of the records, you will then need to go into Modify, and link the records together. But this will automatically be done if you choose the match/merge option. If you haven't already merged them in the temporary working file, you may have three or four records for him that will need to all be merged into one.)

Records uploaded from the International Genealogical Index will not already be linked into families. For example, in the case of James Harvie and his ten children (see Figure 44) you will now have ten children and ten different sets of parents. You want all of the children linked to the same parents. You can do this easily using the match/merge function.

Note: If you have downloaded a large number of records from the International Genealogical Index in one GEDCOM file and have several families with one or both parents having the same names, merging these records is more difficult. You may need to study the records carefully, and perhaps print out reports that will allow you to see them together and perhaps use the RIN (record identification number) to help determine which ones are members of the same family. Viewing the notes, which contain the batch number may also help. It is sometimes helpful

if you made screen prints of the families while you were viewing the records in FamilySearch.

Records that were downloaded from the Social Security Death Index will not be linked to anyone. There is no name of a relative listed in the file. If you download the records of both your father and your mother, you will need to link these together. How this is done is dependent on the circumstances. If you have other records for your parents in the same file, you can simply match/merge the records into the existing ones already linked. But if the file does not already have records for them, you will need to go into the "add a family" function from the Personal Ancestral File Family Records Menu (item 1, see Figure 60, then option 2, and then again option 2), and have the computer "fetch" the records of both and link them as husband and wife. You may want to do this in the temporary file.

The place of birth is not listed in the Social Security Death Index. The place where the person resided when they applied for the Social Security number will be placed in the birth place field in the Personal Ancestral File. You will need to make the needed corrections. (A similar situation exists with the Military Index.)

When you have the records to suit yourself, you will need to create a GEDCOM file (see page 43) and download the records you want to use. This GEDCOM file can be on a diskette, or on the hard drive if it is to be uploaded into the same computer. You can then upload these records into your family records directory and link them into your family records by using the match/merge function, following the same procedures outlined. (See page 43.)

Note: You will need to do two processes here: GEDCOM down the records you want to add to your family records file; and then upload this GEDCOM file to your regular family records file, following the same procedures just outlined, with one exception. To download the GEDCOM file, select option 1 (create GEDCOM File) from the GEDCOM menu (Figure 55) and follow the instructions provided, making sure your "path" shows downloading from the TEMP file [C:\PAF\TEMP].) When that step is completed, select option 2, but change the path (where it says "Family Records Data Disk" in Figure 57) to show your regular family records data file (C:\PAF\NICHOLS, for example), because that is where you are adding these records).

Instructions are also in your user manual for Personal Ancestral File.

For example, you have now added to your family records file the records for the ancestors of James Harvie, born 1746, and linked them by merging the two records you had for him.

In the temporary working file you had...

1. Eliminated the duplication for his son James, born 1773, by linking the records from the Ancestral File (there were two of these--one where he was a child and one where he was a husband). By merging them, you linked his other relatives--his parents and his wife--to his record.

2. You also merged the record where he was listed as Jas. Harvie, father of the children with the document date of his will in 1834. This linked his children to him and his ancestors.

3. Next, you went into the record for each child, and modified it by adding the birth date for each one that you had from other research. You also had an estimated death date for him of 1835. You now want to correct it to the 1834 date. You can do this by

   • Going into the pedigree search (option 4 from the Family Records menu, see Figure 60), placing his name in the principal position as name no. 1 on the pedigree chart, and pressing E (for edit).

   • Making the changes by typing over information that is there, or adding details, and pressing F1.

   • Pressing the 2 key allows you to view the notes also, and then pressing the E for edit, you can make changes in genealogical detail as desired.

   • Pressing the 3 key will allow you to view the marriage information, where you can press the E key to edit the record. Pressing F1 will save the record, and then pressing X will take you back to the pedigree menu.

Try it. It may sound difficult when reading about it, but it realy is not. Just create a temporary data file, and try everything--then enjoy doing it, and show others how!

GLOSSARY
Ancestral File™

A pedigree-linked file of information submitted since 1978 for research and sharing, limited mostly to records of persons who are now deceased. (See page 7.) The 1992 edition (released 1993) on compact disc contains 15 million records. (1992 refers to the date the information was taken from the master file to create the compact disc; the 1993 to the date of distribution.)

Backup

A copy of your automated file that serves as a security copy, in case the data in your regular data file should become damaged.

CD-ROM

A compact disc that can be read by using an addition on a personal computer called a CD-ROM drive, but data cannot be changed. It is similar to a music disc for your CD player.

Compact Disc

A disc similar to a small record, used for storage of large amounts of automated data. It can be used on personal computers with a special attachment called a CD-ROM drive or player.

Directory

In Personal Ancestral File the space identified where the computer will store a file of data.

Diskette

A small disk, either 5 1/4 inches or 3 1/2 inches in size, for storing computerized data. The diskette can be used in personal computers, or to download information from FamilySearch in GEDCOM format which you can take home and use in a personal computer (with the right software program). Also referred to as floppy disk.

There are low density and high density diskettes, which refers to the amount of data the diskette can hold. There are double-sided designations for each—double density (DS DD) refers to the low density ones, while double sided high density (DS HD) does not. Older computers can handle only low density (DS DD) ones, while newer computers can usually handle both. (Computers can, of course, be upgraded from floppy diskettes to a hard disk, or from low density only to handle high density diskettes.)

Download

The process of taking automated records from one computer data base, using a genealogical communications format called GEDCOM, so the records can be added to another computer file without having to retype the information; copy.

Extracted

Entries that were extracted primarily from records of birth, christening, or marriage, where selected pertinent genealogical information was "extracted" from the larger amount of information, and automated. A program to accomplish this is known as the Extraction Program, where volunteers of The Church of Jesus Christ of Latter-day Saints have given many hours to help do this. The *Parish and Vital Records List* (on microfiche) lists the records, localities, and time periods covered, and may indicate whether or not the extracted records are in the current edition of the International Genealogical Index.

FamilySearch[R]

A series of computer programs and data files created by The Church of Jesus Christ of Latter-day Saints, to be run on a personal computer with a CD-ROM drive or player. The files, available on compact disc, include the International Genealogical Index, the Library Catalog, Ancestral File, the U.S. Social Security Death Index, and a Military Index consisting of U.S. citizens who died in Viet Nam and Korea, with others to follow. No modem access presently exists. FamilySearch is presently available mainly at LDS Family History Centers and the main Family History Library in Salt Lake City. It is not generally available for purchase by individuals at this time (January 1994). But sales to individuals is a concept presently being tested.

FamilySearch may be purchased by public libraries, and family history or genealogical organizations from:

GeneSys Genealogical Systems (a division of Dynix)
400 Dynix Dr., P. O. Box 19010
Provo, UT 84605-9010

Freedom of Information Act

A United States law that makes certain types of federal information available to the public. The Social Security Death Index is made available under this Act.

Function Key

A set of keys on the computer keyboard with an F in front of the number. By pressing the key a certain function will be activated; for example, F4 will display the request screen, and F12 will begin a search.

GEDCOM

An abbreviation for Genealogical Data Communications. It formats the data (names, dates, places, linkages, sources, etc) into a form that can be transferred from one computer system to another without having to rekey the information.

There are many programs for personal computers registered with the Family History Department and approved compatible in handling GEDCOM which can communicate with FamilySearch, (in addition to Personal Ancestral File). There are too many to name. You can write for a list, or call for information on any particular program. The FamilySearch support desk can help you.

Please note: in PAF all three options on the Genealogical Information Exchange (GIE) menu create GEDCOM files;
- Ancestral File Submission
- Temple Names Submission
- Genealogical Data Communications (GEDCOM)
Because the first two do not include the term GEDCOM this is sometimes confusing.

Genealogical Resource Files

Large computer files that contain genealogical information which can be accessed as part of FamilySearch, such as Ancestral File and the International Genealogical Index. There are others in process, and it is anticipated that they will be added from time to time.

Given-name Searches

In all files, you can search for individuals who did not have surnames as part of their record by typing only a given name.

In addition, in the International Genealogical Index, for selected countries, you have the option to search for all names arranged by the given name, (the surname is listed but is not part of the sort), and then the event year. This search arranges the given names by standard spelling. This search is provided for countries that used the patronymic naming custom (see glossary entry), such as Denmark, Norway, Sweden, Iceland, and Wales.

Help

In addition to the instructions which always appear on each screen, help messages have been provided for each field on almost every screen as a part of FamilySearch. Press the F1 key while the highlight bar is on that field and the explanation will appear on the screen.

In addition, the Family History Department has published one or more brief guides for each file, such as "Contributing to Ancestral File." These guides may be consulted at Family history centers.

Holding File

A feature in the International Genealogical Index, Social Security Death Index, and Military Index that allows you to place multiple records in temporary storage and either print them or download (copy) them to a diskette as a group.

Import/Export

Terms used only in the MacIntosh version of Personal Ancestral File to refer to adding or downloading GEDCOM records, which is done as part of the Family Records program. (The MacIntosh version of Personal Ancestral File does not have a separate Genealogical Information Exchange program.)

International Genealogical Index™

An index to million of names of deceased persons from nearly a hundred countries, that is produced primarily to assist members of The Church of Jesus Christ of Latter-day Saints to determine if temple ordinances have been performed for their ancestors. It is also an extract of millions of entries taken from vital records, and therefore can be used for research purposes by anyone researching their ancestry. Millions more of the entries come from submissions by relatives, made between the 1840s and 1993. There are two editions: one on microfiche, with the latest edition 1992, and one on compact disc (CD-ROM), with the latest edition 1993 (as of January 1994). The compact disc version is part of FamilySearch (see page 27).

Since the International Genealogical Index (IGI) is so well known in its microfiche version, the following list of differences between the two versions is provided:

1. *Geographical searching*

   On microfiche, the names are arranged alphabetically WITHIN SMALLER LOCALITIES. For example, each state within the United States is separate; each county in England is separate.

   On compact disc, the division is by REGIONS which are larger; for example all of the United States and Canada are one alphabetical listing, which the computer quickly searches for you.

2. *Display of information*

   On compact disc, the names are also arranged by the NAME OF THE PARENT(S). This may bring together brothers and sisters (and others with parents who have the same name(s).

3. *Film number for the source* is listed in the compact disc edition, while for the microfiche version you must consult the IGI Batch Number Index (also on microfiche).

4. *Ease of retrieval.* For the compact disc edition, all you need to do is select a locality and type in a name. The computer takes you to the nearest match. On microfiche, you must use the microfiche reader and locate the entry desired.

5. *Ease of copying.* The compact disc allows you to print an individual record, or place names in a "holding file," and then print them out or download them to a diskette as a group. Microfiche requires using a special machine to make a copy of a single page.

6. *For US and Canada census entries*, the year of birth as well as the year of the census is listed in the compact disc edition.

   Remember on census records (N type) that the PLACE LISTED is where the family was living when the census was taken, NOT THE PLACE OF BIRTH.

7. *Names of places* in the microfiche version are clearly labeled.

   In the compact disc edition, when two levels are given, it is usually the COUNTY and the STATE (or equivalent), but may be the town and state (or province). (This is because some areas do not have counties--such as Alaska, Alberta, British Columbia, Manitoba, Saskatchewan, and Yukon Territory.) This can be confusing if you are not watchful. For example, in such places as Henderson, North Carolina, there is a county named Henderson (which is what is meant when only two levels are displayed.) There is also a town, located in another county: Henderson in Vance County.

   If the town is referenced in an entry, all three levels would be displayed.

   Please note: In the 1988 edition, the content of the index (with the exception of the added microfilm numbers for the source documents) was exactly the same between the two editions. However, now the 1992 edition (with 187 million names) is published only on microfiche; the 1993 edition (with over 200 million names) is published only on compact disc.

Family History Library Catalog

A listing of all of the records in the collection of the Family History Library in Salt Lake City, most of which can be ordered and used at the family history centers. There are two editions: one on microfiche, and one on compact disc (CD-ROM). The compact disc version is part of FamilySearch. One compact disc contains the descriptions of all the records in the library. You can search by (1) locality, (2) surname, or (3) film or fiche library call number. It is not possible yet to search by author or title in the compact disc version.

Mailing Address

Submissions of automated data in GEDCOM format should be mailed to: Ancestral File, Family History Department, 50 East North Temple Street, Salt Lake City, Utah 84150.

Menu

In a computer software program, a list of options from which to choose. Pressing ENTER while the highlight bar is on the desired item or pressing the alphabetical letter beside the option will tell the computer what you want to do.

Military Index

An index of United States Citizens who died in Viet Nam and Korea during military service, on compact disc. The information comes from the U.S. government, and is made available through the Freedom of Information Act.

Name-Only

The name of a person in Ancestral file which was submitted without any dates or places, because there was no space on the submission form for these details. The name was part of the record of the child or spouse, and no Ancestral File record was created in the first edition (1989) of the compact discs. These entries were later made into records with estimated dates and places, and linked to the record of the child or spouse. There were approximately two and one-half million of these entries. (See page 14.)

Parent Index

An arrangement of records in the International Genealogical Index on compact disc listing the parent(s) names in alphabetical order, followed by the names of the children listed in chronological order of birth or christening. (See page 30.)

Path

In Personal Ancestral File the detailed description of where a file of data is stored by the computer. For example, it may be stored on drive C, within a subdirectory named PAF, in a directory named HARVIE: C:\PAF\HARVIE. (See Figures 51 and 52.)

Patronymic

A naming custom where the surname (last name) changes every generation, based on the given name of the father. For example, Jens Nielsen is the son of Niels, and his children will be named Jensen. The term Datter is often used for girls, for example, Catherine Jensdatter. (The Scandinavian spelling of Datter [Jensdatter] will retrieve names in FamilySearch, but the American spelling of DAUGHTER [Jensdaughter] will not.

Personal Ancestral File® (PAF)

A package of computer programs to be used on a personal computer, allowing you to type in names, dates, and places and have them linked into families—for pedigrees, family groups, and other reports. Also includes a program called Genealogical Information Exchange, which includes Genealogical Data Communications (GEDCOM) enabling you to download and upload data from and to other files and programs without rekeying the information. Published by The Church of Jesus Christ of Latter-day Saints; available to anyone at the low cost of $35 from LDS Church Distribution Centers. The address of the Salt Lake Distribution Center is 1999 West 1700 South, Salt Lake City, Utah 84104. The current version for the MS-DOS (IBM and compatible) is 2.3 available on either 5 1/4 or 3 1/2 " diskettes; for MacIntosh, version 2.1. (Apple II version 2.0 has been discontinued and there is no Apple II version available. Those having Apple II 2.0 can still download GEDCOM records to submit to Ancestral File, but cannot upload FamilySearch records.) Only the MS-DOS version is completely updated. Illustrations in this pamphlet are using the MS DOS 2.2 and 2.3 versions. The Personal Ancestral File software can be used to submit names for Ancestral File, and to TempleReady for LDS members.

User Groups. Several user groups have developed across the country, where users are helping each other in learning to make better use of Personal Ancestral File, as well as in programming add-on utilities to enhance its functionality. Some groups have contacted the Family History Department Support Group in Salt Lake City and provide help under their guidance. The local groups also serve to provide input for future versions of Personal Ancestral File and as testers for software enhancements and changes.

For a list of user groups in your area, write to Personal Ancestral File, 50 East North Temple Street, Salt Lake City, UT 84150.

Places

Places are always listed with the smallest level to the largest. (Example: parish, town, county, state or country)

In the International Genealogical Index the term *Twp* is an abreviation for township. (This sometimes apears when there was actually no township for that area.)

The abreviation *MN* is a state abbreviation listed in Ancestral File. Normally it refers to Minnesota. However, occasionally it refers instead to Maine. Some years ago the Family History Department had a method of abbreviating names of counties and states or countries which took the first letter of the name and then up to the first six constants (dropping all vowels). MN was for Maine in that old system. Some of the records coming into Ancestral File are being copied from those old records, by submitters. When MN should refer to Maine, a correction needs to be made.

(There are other odd-looking abbreviations that are carry-overs from these old abbreviations, such as N-SC for Nova Scotia or S-LK for Salt Lake county. These are all copied from the old forms, and need to have the place names corrected. However, MN is the only one that now refers to a different place.)

Printout

A paper copy of a report from a computer. For example, a pedigree chart or family group record printed from Ancestral File are printouts.

Royalty and Medieval Records

Records for families of kings (legitimate and illegitimate offspring) and for persons born earlier than 1500, with many other affiliated records, are being compiled by volunteers under direction of the Medieval Identification Unit of the Family History Department. Many of these records have been added to Ancestral File.

Often they have also been submitted by others, using varying names, dates, and places and therefore have not merged correctly with existing records in the file.

In addition, some genealogical dates with only three digits (890, for example), were discarded by the computer and replaced with the LDS ordinance dates. Many of these have been corrected. You may occasionally find a person whose spouse was born in 870, but whose record says they are LIVING. Be patient until all of these can be identified and corrected.

Before you submit any records on persons who may be considered part of royal families, or are pre-1500, please check Ancestral File to see if the records are already there. You will need to search using a number of possible names and spellings (see below, and page 4). It would also be helpful if you contacted the Medieval Identification Unit, 50 East North Temple Street, Salt Lake City, Utah 84150 to coordinate efforts and obtain guidelines before you submit.

The names of royalty may be listed differently from what you expect to find. For example, the name of the country where the individual was a member of a royal family is used as the surname. ENGLAND is the surname for the kings, queens, princes and princesses of that country; SCOTLAND, ITALY, FRANCE, and other countries are also used as surnames. To find such records in Ancestral File, type in the name of the country in the surname field. Other names are found under their English, French, or other language spelling. (The term "Concubine" is used when the mother was not a legal wife of the father, and her name is not known.)

Social Security Death Index (U.S.)

An index of names with brief details of persons who had Social Security numbers and whose deaths were reported to the Social Security office between the years of 1962-1988 (with a few earlier and later). It is made available through the Freedom of Information Act. (See page 39.)

Upload

Taking automated records that have been downloaded from one computerized file and adding them to another computer file without retyping the information.

Version

Similar to edition, it is used with software. For example, Personal Ancestral File 2.2 means this is a version identified as 2.2., which is different (has additional features and functions) from version 2.1, or 2.0.

INDEX

Index to Illustrations

CHANGES TO FAMILYSEARCH

For those who have previously used FamilySearch or any of its files, the following major changes are summarized:

Ancestral File

1. The amount of data has greatly increased. The edition that is currently available includes data submitted through August 1992, with diskette corrections (created by using the F3 edit key) and corrections made through the Administrative system through January 1993.

There are 15 million records in this edition of Ancestral File.

2. There are various other refinements that make using the file easier, such as: when downloading records, a screen will tell you how many direct-line families accompany a pedigree chart (allowing you to gauge the amount of time required to download their records), another display tells you what percentage of the file has been downloaded (allowing you to know how nearly complete the task is), a major reduction in the number of disc swaps required to retrieve a pedigree and the supporting families, etc. However, such very helpful additions do not change the instruction given in this publication.

The International Genealogical Index (IGI)

The instruction in this publication refers to the 1993 edition of the International Genealogical Index (IGI). The 1992 edition was published only on microfiche, and the 1993 edition is available only on compact disc. Watch for updates--in whatever format they may be made available.

The following information outlines major changes in the International Genealogical Index since the 1988 edition:

1. Number of entries. The 1988 edition contained 147 million names. The 1992 edition (on microfiche only) contains 187 million names; the 1993 edition contains more than 200 million names.

New types of records added:
- Pre-1970 LDS Temple records- 24.5 million (13 million proxy baptisms, 1840-1942; 11.5 million proxy endowments, 1942-1969, includes official baptism date).

- Names with incomplete identifiers submitted 1978-1990, 4.5 million (F batch no. prefix).

- Names submitted by relatives since 1990, 10 million.

2. Regions are grouped differently. This applied to differences between the 1988 compact disc, the 1992 microfiche and the 1993 compact disc editions. The compact disc regions are larger, but can be filtered to smaller areas (No change here. In many countries you can filter to the county level, but not in the United States, for example--only to the state level there.)

3. Standard spellings of surnames use an improved formula from that used in 1988 or 1992 for the United States and Canada (North America) region. Some names that used be retrieved under one standard spelling will not to be retrieved, while others not previously included will be retrieved. Try other spellings when expected records are not displayed.

Surnames beginning with Mac, Mc, M' are handled well in the newer editions bringing all (or most) spelling variations together. Other names that can be written with or without a space can still present a challenge. For example, Dewees, Deweese, De Wees, and De Weese are all the same family. Dewees and Deweese spellings are now brought together, but if there is space between the De and Weese, entries are not retrieved with those without a space.

4. The 1993 compact disc edition has standard spellings for given names. For example, it brings together names such as Catherine, Katherine and William, Wm. (but, Bill and Billy are not retrieved with William.) It is a great help, but it is not yet perfect.

5. The 1993 compact disc edition has separate listings for marriages (LDS sealing-to-spouse records) and other events. Thus, there is no longer a single listing of all names in the IGI. (The parent index display still arranges records of individual events [births, christenings, miscellaneous, etc] by the names of the parent(s).)

6. Names are filed differently in the 1993 edition: (1) surname, (2) first given name, and (3) event date. This ignores the middle given name or initial. (This is different from Ancestral File.)

Mr., Miss, and Mrs. are ignored in all editions. Mrs. Martha Jones is filed under Martha Jones, and Mrs. is displayed. If there is no given name, such as Mrs. Jones, the name appears at the beginning of the surname listing with other entries that have no given name.

7. Some additional filters are available. See page 33.